WOODROW WILSON'S
CASE FOR THE LEAGUE
OF NATIONS

Compiled with his approval

By

HAMILTON FOLEY

PRINCETON
PRINCETON UNIVERSITY PRESS
LONDON: HUMPHREY MILFORD
OXFORD UNIVERSITY PRESS
MCMXXIII

PRINTED AT THE PRINCETON UNIVERSITY PRESS
Princeton New Jersey, United States of America

TO FRANCES

CONTENTS

A letter from Woodrow Wilson

WOODROW WILSON
WASHINGTON D C

26th April 1923

My dear Mr. Foley,

      I congratulate you upon the
completion of a difficult piece of work, and I
confidently hope that the book will be of service
to all who wish to understand the League of Nations
and the vital issues which arise out of the attitude
of the United States towards the League.

      As I have written you before, I could not
consent to have the book appear as my own, but
if you will publish it with a frank statement
on the title page of what it is and how it was
made, it will have my entire approval.

      Sincerely Yours,

Woodrow Wilson

Mr. Hamilton Foley,
Pittsburg, Penna.

THIS BOOK

"... a frank statement ... of what
it is and how it was made."

THIS is a compilation of President Wilson's
official and detailed explanation of the League
of Nations Covenant and of the Treaty of
Versailles, made to the Foreign Relations
Committee of the Senate, and to the people of
the United States, when the Treaty was before the Senate in 1919.

To this has been appended, in full, the Covenant and two Addresses he delivered before
the Peace Conference at Paris. One in which
he made it clear the United States had no intention of entering the politics of Europe and
was concerned primarily for the peace of the
world. The other in which he explained the
Covenant of the existing League of Nations.

His explanation to the Senators, was given
at a Conference with them, at the White
House, in August 1919. His explanation to
the people, was given in some thirty-seven
Addresses delivered during his tour of the
Western States in the month of September
following.

From the stenographic minutes of that
White House Conference and from the official
record of all of those Addresses to the public,

I have taken sentences pertaining to each section of the Treaty and of the League, to World Problems and to World Peace, of which he made mention, and so combined them that within the pages of this book may be found President Wilson's personal, comprehensive and detailed explanation of all phases of the questions he put before the people in all of his Addresses; and, so far as circumstances permitted, in his Conference with the Members of the Senate Committee on Foreign Relations.

Every word in this book is Mr. Wilson's own word, and all are here used in explanation of that detail of the subject in which he used them.

Explaining the Treaty of Versailles, President Wilson spoke with the full knowledge and authority that came to him as the War President of this country; as the official spokesman, by their request, for the Allied and Associated Powers in the pre-Armistice negotiations with the Central Powers, and as one of the four or five Members of the Peace Conference that had it within their power to influence in the greatest degree the policies of the peace.

Explaining the League of Nations, President Wilson spoke with the knowledge and authority that came to him as Chairman of the Commission on the League of Nations o the Peace Conference. As Chairman of that Commission, President Wilson was the first to present and explain the existing Covenant to the representatives of all the Nations of the world at the Paris Peace Conference. As Chairman of that Commission, he gave the Peace Conference, as a whole, the first official knowledge of the way its purposes and policies for permanent world peace had been written into the Covenant.

After hearing President Wilson's explanation of the attitude of the United States toward a League of Nations, and his explanation of the Covenant of the existing League, all the Nations at the Paris Peace Conference unanimously adopted the Covenant as it now exists. Assured and convinced, these other countries have since joined the League: Albania, Argentine Republic, Austria, Bulgaria, Chile, Colombia, Costa Rica, Denmark, Esthonia, Finland, Hungary, Latvia, Lithuania, Luxemburg, Netherlands, Norway, Paraguay, Persia, Salvador, Spain, Sweden, Switzerland, Venezuela.

These facts make these explanations of Woodrow Wilson as to the League of Nations, a part of the Diplomatic and War History of all the Nations of the world.

While Mr. Wilson has generously given this compilation his entire approval, I wish to assume, personally, all the responsibility for any possible error in quotation that may have passed unnoticed and without intention. My one thought and purpose has been to make available the complete and authoritative explanation of the League of Nations, and all that it means for the peace of the world, made by the President of the United States who presided at the formation of the Covenant of the League, and whose explanation of it has been officially accepted by practically every Government in the world.

HAMILTON FOLEY

Pittsburgh, Pa.

WOODROW WILSON'S
CASE FOR THE LEAGUE
OF NATIONS

THE WORLD WAR

THE people of the United States have not been informed of the real character and scope and contents of the great Treaty of peace with Germany, which we shall always know as the Treaty of Versailles. The people of the United States have been singularly and I sometimes fear deliberately, misled as to the Treaty of peace. In the greater part of the United States the people do not know what is in the Treaty.

They have been directed to certain points in the Treaty which are incidental and not central. Their attention has been drawn away from the real meaning of this great document, and I think I cannot do you a better service, or the peace of the world a better service, than by pointing out to you just what this Treaty contains and what it seeks to do, because we are now as a Nation to make what I cannot help characterizing as the most critical decision we have ever made in the history of America.

In order to check the falsehoods that have clustered around this great subject I want to tell you a few very simple things about the Treaty and the Covenant.

THE WORLD WAR

We sent our boys across the sea to defeat the purpose of Germany, but we engaged that after we had defeated the purposes of Germany we would complete what they had begun and effect such arrangements of international concert as would make it impossible for any such attempt ever to be made again. The question therefore is, "Shall we see it through or shall we now at this most critical juncture of the whole transaction turn away from our associates in the war and decline to complete and fulfill our sacred promise to mankind."

I want, if you will be patient with me, to set the stage for the Treaty, to let you see just what it was that was meant to be accomplished and just what it was that was accomplished.

Perhaps I can illustrate better by recalling some history.

Something over a hundred years ago the last so-called peace conference sat at Vienna,—back in the far year 1815, if I remember correctly. It was made up, as the recent conference in Paris was, of the leading statesmen of Europe. America was not then drawn into that general family and was not represented at that conference, and practically every government represented at that time, except the Government of Great Britain, was a government like the recent Government of Germany, where a small coterie of autocrats were able to determine the fortunes of their people without consulting them, were able to use their people as puppets and pawns in the game of ambition which was being played all over the stage in Europe.

But just before that conference there had been many signs that there was a breaking up of that old order, there had been some ominous signs indeed. It was not then so long ago, though there were but three million people subject to the Crown of Great Britain in America, they had thrown off allegiance to that Crown successfully and defied the power of the British Empire on the ground that nobody at a distance had a right to govern them whom they did not choose to be their government; founding their government upon the principle that all just government rests upon the consent of the governed. And there had followed, as you remember, that whirlwind of passion that we know as the French Revolution, when all the foundations of French Government not only, but of French society, had been shaken and disturbed—a great rebellion of a great suffering population against an intolerable authority that had laid all the taxes on the poor and none of them on the rich, that had used the people as servants, that had made the boys and men of France play upon the battle field as if they were chessmen upon a board. France revolted and then the spirit spread, and the conference at Vienna was intended to check the revolutionary spirit of the time. These men met in order to concert methods by which they could make monarchs and monarchies safe, not only in Europe but throughout the world.

The British representatives at that conference were alarmed because they heard it whispered that European governments, European monarchies, particularly those of the center of Europe, those of Austria and Germany—for Austria was then stronger than Germany— were purposing to extend their power to the Western hemisphere, to the Americas, and the prime minister of Great Britain suggested to Mr. Rush, the minister of the United States at the Court of Great Britain, that he put it in the ear of Mr. Monroe who was then President, that this thing was afoot and that it might be profitable to say something about it. Thereupon, Mr. Monroe uttered his famous Monroe Doctrine, saying that European power that sought either to colonize this Western Hemisphere or to interfere with its political institutions, or to extend monarchial institutions to it, would be regarded as having done an unfriendly act to the United States, and since then no power has dared interfere with the self-determination of the Americas.

That is the famous Monroe Doctrine. We love it because it was the first effective dam built up against the tide of autocratic power. The men who constituted the Congress of Vienna, while they thought they were building of adamant were building of cardboard. What they threw up looked like battlements but presently were blown down by the very breath of insurgent people, for all over Europe during the middle of the last century there spread, spread irresistibly, the spirit of revolution. Government after government was changed in its character. People said, "It is not only in America that men want to govern themselves, it is not only in France that men mean to throw off this intolerable yoke. All men are of the same temper and of the same make and of the same rights." So the tide of revolution could not be stopped by the conclusions of the Congress of Vienna, until it came about that there was only one stronghold left for that sort of power, and that was at Berlin.

In the year 1914 that power sought to make reconquest of Europe and the world. It was nothing less than the re-assertion of that old, ugly thing which the hearts of men everywhere always revolt against—the claim of a few men to determine the fortunes of all men,

the ambition of little groups of rulers to dominate the world, the plots and intrigues of military staffs and men who did not confide in
their fellow citizens what it was that was their
ultimate purpose. Up to the time of this war,
it was the firm and fixed conviction of the
statesmen in Europe that the greater nations
ought to dominate and guide and determine
the destiny of the weaker nations, and the
American principle was rejected. The American principle is that, just as the weak man
has the same legal rights that the strong man
has, just as the poor man has the same rights
as the rich, though I am sorry to say he does
not always get them, so as between nations the
principle of equality is the only principle of
justice, and the weak nations have just as
many rights and just the same rights as the
strong nations.

I want to recall to you the circumstances of
the war and the purposes for which our men
spent their lives on the other side of the sea.
That war did not just happen. There was not
some sudden occasion which brought on a
conflagration. On the contrary Germany had
been preparing for that war for generations.
Germany had been preparing every resource,
perfecting every skill, developing every invention, which would enable her to master the
European world; and after mastering the

European world, to dominate the rest of the world. Everybody had been looking on. Everybody had known. For example, it was known in every war office in Europe, and in the War Department at Washington, that the Germans not only had a vast supply of great field guns but that they had ammunition enough for every one of those guns to exhaust the gun. Yet we were all living in a fool's paradise. We thought that Germany meant what she said—that she was armed for defense; that she would never use that great store of force against the rest of her fellow men. Why, it was foreordained the minute Germany conceived these purposes that she should do the thing which she did in 1914.

What happened? You will remember that a Prince of the House of Austria was slain in one of the cities of Serbia. Not assassinated by anybody over whom the Government of Serbia had any control, but assassinated by some man who had in his heart the memory of something that was intolerable to him, that had been done to the people that he belonged to. Serbia was one of the little kingdoms of Europe. She had no strength which any of the great powers needed to fear, and as we see the war now, Germany and those who conspired with her made a pretext of that assassination to make unconscionable demands of the weak and helpless Kingdom of Serbia. Not with a view to bringing about an acquiescence in those demands, but with a view to bringing about a conflict in which other purposes quite separate from the purposes connected with these demands could be achieved. Poor Serbia, in her sudden terror, with the memory of things that had happened before and might happen again, practically yielded to every demand, and with regard to a little portion of the ultimatum said she would like to talk it over with them, and they did not dare to wait.

Just as soon as these demands were made on Serbia the other Governments of Europe sent telegraphic messages to Berlin and Vienna asking that the matter be brought into conference, and the significant circumstance of the beginning of this war is that the Austrian and German Governments did not dare to discuss the demands on Serbia or the purposes which they had in view. You dare not lay a bad case before mankind. It is universally admitted on the other side of the water that if they had gone into international conference on the Austrian demands the war never would have been begun. There was an insistent demand from London, for example, by the British foreign minister, that the Cabinets of Europe should be allowed time to confer with the Governments of Vienna and Berlin so as to see if war could not be avoided, and the Governments at Vienna and Berlin did not dare admit time for discussion.

You will remember how the conscience of mankind was shocked by what Germany did; not merely by the circumstances to which I have already adverted, that unconscionable demands were made upon a little nation which could not resist, but that immediately upon the beginning of the war the solemn engagements of treaty were cast on one side, and the chief representative of the Imperial Government of Germany said that when national purposes were under consideration treaties were mere scraps of paper; and immediately upon that declaration, the German armies invaded the territories of Belgium which they had engaged should be inviolate, invaded those territories with the half-avowed purpose that Belgium was necessary to be permanently retained by Germany in order that she should have the proper frontage on the sea and the proper advantage in her contest with the other nations of the world. So that the act which was characteristic of the beginning of this war was a violation of the territorial integrity of the Kingdom of Belgium.

The world did not realize in 1914 that it had come to the final grapple of principle. The old order of things the rest of the world seemed to have got, in some sense, used to. The old order of things was not to depend upon the general moral judgment of mankind, not to base policies upon international right, but to base policies upon international power. So there were drawn together groups of nations which stood armed, facing one another, which stood drawing their power from the vitality of people who did not wish to be subordinated to them, drawing their vitality from the energy of great peoples who did not wish to devote their energy to force, but wished to devote their energy to peace. The world thought it was inevitable. This group of nations thought that it represented one set of principles, that group of nations thought that it represented another set of principles, and that the best that could be accomplished in the world was this that they used to call the balance of power.

Notice the phrase! Not the balance that you try to maintain in a court of justice, not the scales of justice, but the scales of force; one great force balanced against another force. Every bit of the policy of the world, internationally speaking, was made in the interest of some national advantage on the part of the stronger nations of the world. It was either the advantage of Germany or the advantage of Great Britain or the advantage of Italy or

the advantage of Japan. We thought that the
cool spaces of the ocean on the east and west
of us would keep us from the infections that
came, arising like miasmatic mists, out of that
arrangement of power and of suspicion and of
dread.

The only people in Europe who instinctive-
ly realized what was going to happen and did
happen in 1914 was the French people. For
nearly fifty years, ever since the settlement
which took Alsace-Lorraine away from them
in 1871, they had expected it. For nearly fifty
years they had dreaded by the exercise of
German force the very thing that happened.
But the other nations took it lightly. There
were wise men in Great Britain, there were
wise men in the United States, who pointed
out to us not only what they suspected, but
what we all knew with regard to the prepara-
tions for the use of force in Europe. Nobody
was ignorant of what Germany was doing.
What we shut our eyes against deliberately
was the probability that she would make the
use of her preparation that she did finally
make of it. Her military men published books
and told us what they were going to do with
it, but we dismissed them. We said, "The
thing is a nightmare. The man is a crank. It
cannot be that he speaks for a great Government!" Very well, could it not happen? Did

it not happen? Are we satisfied now what the balance of power means? It means that the stronger force will sometimes be exercised or an attempt be made to exercise it to crush the other powers.

It was only by slow degrees that we realized that we had any part in the war. We started the forces in 1776, as I have said, that made this war inevitable, but we were a long time realizing that, after all, that was what was at issue. We had been accustomed to regarding Europe as a field of intriguing, of rival ambitions, and of attempts to establish empire, and at first we merely got the impression that this was one of the usual European wars, to which, unhappily, mankind had become only too accustomed. You know how unwilling we were to go into it. I can speak for myself. I made every effort to keep this country out of the war, until it came to my conscience, as it came to yours, that after all it was our war as well as Europe's war, that the ambition of these central empires was directed against nothing less than the liberty of the world. We tried to convince ourselves that no matter what happened on the other side of the sea, no obligation of duty rested upon us, and finally we found the currents of humanity too strong for us. We found that a great consciousness was welling up in us that this was not a local cause, that this was not a struggle that was to be confined to Europe, or confined to Asia, to which it had spread, but that it was something that involved the very fate of civilization; that there was one great nation in the world that could not afford to stay out of it.

We were caught in this thing by the action of a nation utterly unlike ourselves. What I mean to say is that the German nation, the German people, had no choice whatever as to whether it was to go into that war or not, did not know that it was going into it until its men were summoned to the colors. I remember not once, but often, sitting at the Cabinet table in Washington, I asked my colleagues what their impression was of the opinion of the country before we went into the war, and I remember one day one of my colleagues said to me, "Mr. President, I think the people of the country would take your advice and do what you suggested." "Why," I said, "that is not what I am waiting for; that is not enough. If they cannot go in with a whoop, there is no use of their going in at all. I do not want them to wait on me. I am waiting on them. I want to know what the conscience of this country is speaking. I want to know what the purpose is arising in the minds of the people of this country with regard to this world situation. I must wait until I know that I am interpreting their purpose, then I will know that I have got an irresistible power behind me." And that is exactly what happened! When I thought I heard that voice, it was then that I proposed to the Congress of the United States that we should include ourselves in the challenge that Germany was giving to mankind.

That is what is now appreciated as it was not at first appreciated on the other side of the sea. They wondered and wondered why we did not come in. They had come to the rather cynical conclusion that we did not come in because we were making money out of this war, and did not want to spoil the profitable game; and then at last they saw what we were waiting for—in order that the whole plot of the German purpose should develop, in order that we might see how the intrigue of that plot had penetrated our own life, how the poison was spreading, and how it was nothing less than a design against the freedom of the world.

Until we went into this war, it was the al-.most universal impression of the world that our idealism was a mere matter of words; that what we were interested in was getting on in the world and making as much as we should out of it. That was the sum and substance of the usual opinion of us outside of America; and in the short space that we were in this war that opinion was absolutely reversed. Consider what they saw! The flower of our youth sent three and four thousand miles away from their homes, a home which could not be directly touched by the flames of that war, sent to foreign fields to mix with foreign and alien armies to fight for a cause which they recognized as the common cause of mankind, and not the peculiar cause of America! It caused a revulsion of feeling, a revulsion of attitude which I dare say, has never been parallelled in the world.

AMERICAN SOLDIERS IN EUROPE

We went in just in time. The hope of Europe had sunk very low when American troops began to throng overseas. One of the most beautiful stories I know is the story that we heard in France about the first effect of the American soldiers when they got over there. The French did not believe at first, the British did not believe, that we could finally get 2,000,000 over there. The most that they hoped at first was that a few American soldiers would restore their morale, for let me say their morale was gone. The beautiful story to which I referred is this—the testimony that all of them rendered that they got their morale back the minute they saw the eyes of those boys! There was no curtain in front of the retina of those eyes! They were American eyes! There was something in their eyes they had never seen in the eyes of any other army—the feeling that penetrates every American, that there is a great future, that a man can handle his own fortunes, that it is his right to have his place in the world, and that no man that he does not choose is his master! That is what these people saw in the eyes of the American boys who carried their arms across the sea. There was America in every one of those lively eyes, and America was not looking merely at the fields of France, was not merely seeking to defeat Germany; she was seeking to defeat everything that Germany's action represented, and to see to it that there never happened such a thing again!

You remember what happened in that fateful battle in which our men first took part. You remember how the French lines had been beaten and separated and broken at Chateau-Thierry, and you remember how the gates seemed open for the advancement of the Germans upon Paris. Then a body of men, a little body of men—American soldiers and American Marines—against the protests of French officers, against the command of the remote commanders, nevertheless dared to fill that breach, stopped that advance, turned the Germans back, and never allowed them to turn their faces forward again. They were advised to go back, and they asked the naive American question, "What did we come over here for? We did not come over here to go back! We came over here to go forward!" "We didn't come over here to wait, we came over here to fight!" and their very audacity, their very indifference to danger, changed the morale of the battle field. They were not fighting prudently; they were going to get there! And they never went in any other direction! The men who went to Chateau-Thierry, the men who went into Belleau Wood, the men who did what no other troops had been able to do in the Argonne, never thought of turning back. They had gone to Europe to go the whole way toward the realization of the teaching which their fathers had handed down to them. There never were crusaders that went to the Holy Land in the old ages that we read about that were more truly devoted to a holy cause than these gallant, incomparable sons of America.

Ask this question of yourselves, mothers and fathers and wives and sweethearts, who sent their beloved young men to France. What did you send them there for? What made you proud that they were going? What made you willing that they should go? Did you think that they were going to aggrandize

America in some way? It is not a handsome enterprise for any great nation to go into a war merely to reduce another nation to obedience! Did you think that they were going to take something for America that had belonged to somebody else? Did you think they were going in a quarrel which they had provoked and must maintain? It is so easy, with the strong tides of our life, to be swept away from one situation into another and to forget the real depths of meaning which lie underneath the things that we are merely touching the surface of. Therefore, it might be useful if I remind you of a few things, lest we forget,—if I asked permission to read you the concluding passage of the address in which I requested the Government of the United States to accept Germany's challenge of war:

"We shall fight," I said, "for the things "which we have always carried nearest our "hearts, for democracy, for the right of those "who submit to authority to have a voice in "their own governments, for the rights and lib-"erties of small nations, for a universal domin-"ion of right by such a concert of free peoples "as will bring peace and safety to all nations "and make the world itself at last free. To such "a task we can dedicate our lives and our for-"tunes, everything that we are and everything "that we have, with the pride of those who "know that the day has come when America is "privileged to spend her blood and her might "for the principles that gave her birth and the "happiness and the peace which we have treas-"ured. God helping her, she can do no other."

That is the program we started out on. That is the program which all America adopted without respect of party, and shall we now hesitate to carry it out?

You were proud that they should go because they were going on an errand of self-sacrifice, in the interest of mankind. This sacrifice was made in order that other sons should not be called upon for a similar gift, the gift of life, the gift of all that died. These men were crusaders. They were not going forth to prove the might of the United States. They were going forth to prove the might of justice and of right, and all the world accepted them as crusaders, and their transcendent achievement has made all the world believe in America as it believed in no other nation organized in the modern world. We were a long time seeing that we belonged in the war, but just as soon as the real issues of it became apparent we knew that we belonged there. We did an unprecedented thing. We threw the whole power of a great nation into a quarrel with the origination of which it had nothing to do.

Let us never forget those years. Let us never

forget the purpose—the high purpose, the disinterested purpose—with which America lent its strength, not for its own glory but for the defense of mankind. I think there is nothing that appeals to the imagination more in the history of men than those convoyed fleets crossing the ocean with the millions of American soldiers aboard—those crusaders, those men who loved liberty enough to leave their homes and fight for them upon the distant fields of battle, those men who swung into the open as if in fulfillment of the long prophecy of American history.

What a halo and glory surrounds those old men whom we now greet with such reverence, the men who were the soldiers in our Civil War! They saved a Nation! When these youngsters grow old who have come back from the fields of France, what a halo will be around their brows! They saved the world! They are of the same stuff as those old veterans of the Civil War. I was born and bred in the South, but I can pay that tribute with all my heart to the men who saved the Union. It ought to have been saved! It was the greatest thing that men had conceived up to that time. Now we come to a greater thing—to the union of great nations in conference upon the interests of peace. That is the fruitage, the fine and appropriate fruitage of what these men achieved upon fields of France. I do not hesitate to say, as a sober interpretation of history, that American soldiers saved the liberties of the world.

Shall the great sacrifice that we made in this war be in vain, or shall it not? It is very important that we should not forget what this war meant. I am amazed at the indications that on the other side of the water they are apt to forget what they went through. In order that we may not forget, I brought (give) the figures as to what this war meant to the world. If I did not have them on official authority I would deem them incredible. They are too big for the imagination of men who do not handle big things. Here is the cost of the war in money, exclusive of what we loaned one another—a grand total of direct war costs of $186,000,000,000—almost the capital of the world. The expenditures of the United States were at the rate of a million dollars an hour for two years, including night-time with day-time! The battle deaths during the war, the total for all the belligerents was 7,450,000—just about seven and a half million killed. The totals for wounded are not obtainable except our own. Our own wounded were 230,000, excluding those who were killed. The total of all battle deaths in all the wars from the year 1793 to 1914 was something under 6,000,000 men, so that about a million and a half more men were killed in this war than in all the wars of something more than one hundred preceding years. These are terrible facts and we ought never to forget them.

This nation went into this war to see it through to the end, and the end has not come yet. This is the beginning not of the war, but of the processes which are going to render a war like this impossible. The past is only a prediction of the future, and all this terrible thing that your brothers and husbands and sweethearts have been through may have to be gone through with again.

The task, that great and gallant task, which our soldiers performed is only half finished. Their part was the negative part merely. They were sent over there to see that a malign influence did not interfere with the just fortunes of the world. They stopped that influence, but they did not accomplish anything constructive. They prevented a great wrong. They prevented it with a spirit and a courage and with an ability that will always be written on the brightest pages of our record of gallantry and of force. I do not know when I have been as proud, as an American, as when I have seen our boys deploy on the other side of the sea. On Christmas day, on an open stretch of country, I saw a great Division[1] march past me, with all the arms of the service, walking with that swing which is so familiar to our eyes, with that sense of power and confidence and audacity which is so characteristic of America, and I seemed to see the force that had saved the world! But they merely prevented something. They merely prevented a particular nation from doing a particular, unspeakable wrong to civilization, and their task is not complete unless we see to it that it has not to be done over again, unless we fulfill the promise which we made to them and to ourselves that this was not only a war to defeat Germany, but a war to prevent the recurrence of any such wrong as Germany had attempted; that it was a war to put an end to the wars of aggression forever.

We undertook a great war for a definite purpose. That definite purpose is carried out in a great Treaty. While victory has been won, it has been won only over the force of a particular group of nations. It has not been won over the passions of those nations, or over the passions of the nations that were set against them. This Treaty tries to deal with some of the elements of passion which were likely at

[1]A composite Divison of troops from the 26th, 29th, 77th, 80th and 82nd Divisions, Major General Robert Alexander, Commanding.

any time to blaze out in the world and which did blaze out and set the world on fire. And do not believe that civilization is saved now. There were passions let loose upon the field of the world by that war which have not grown quiet yet, which will not grow quiet for a long time. The harness that is to unite nations is more necessary now than it ever was before, and unless there is this assurance of combined action before wrong is attempted, wrong will be attempted just as soon as the most ambitious nations can recover from the financial stress of this war.

The completion of the work of those men is this, that the thing that they fought to stop shall never be attempted again. There seems to me to stand between us and the rejection or qualification of this Treaty the serried ranks of those dear boys in khaki, not only those boys who came home, but those dear ghosts that still deploy upon the fields of France.

THE TREATY OF VERSAILLES

I AM going to try to point out some of the things that are the salient and outstanding characteristics of this Treaty.

I have no hesitation in saying that in spirit and essence it is an American document, and if you will bear with me, for this is a subject for examination and discussion, I will remind you of some of the things that we have long desired and which are at last accomplished in this Treaty.

The Treaty begins with the Covenant of the League of Nations, which is intended to operate as a partnership, a permanent partnership, of the great and free self-governing peoples of the world to stand sponsor for the right and for civilization. Notice is given in the very first articles of the Treaty that hereafter it will not be a matter of conjecture whether the other great nations of the world will combine against a wrongdoer, but a matter of certainty that hereafter nations contemplating what the Government of Germany contemplated will not have to conjecture whether Great Britain and France and Italy and the great United States will join hands against them, but will know that mankind, in serried ranks, will defend to the last the rights of human beings wherever they are. By common consent that was put first, because by common consent, without it the Treaty cannot be worked, and without it, it is a mere temporary arrangement with Germany.

I am not going to speak here particularly of the Covenant of the League of Nations. I am going to point out to you what the Treaty as a whole is.

It is a document unique in the history of the world for many reasons, and one of the things that made it great was that it was penetrated throughout with the principles to which America has devoted her life. Let me hasten to say that one of the most delightful circumstances of the work on the other side of the water was that I discovered what we called American principles had penetrated to the heart and to the understanding not only of the great peoples of Europe but to the hearts and understandings of the great men who were leading the peoples of Europe, and when these principles were written into this Treaty, they were written there by common consent and common conviction, but it remains true nevertheless, that principles were written into that Treaty which were never written into any great international understanding before, and that they had their natural birth and origin in this dear country to which we have devoted our life and service.

In the first place, it seeks to punish one of the greatest wrongs in history, the wrong which Germany sought to do to the world and to civilization. The thing that Germany attempted, if it had succeeded, would have set the civilization of the world back a hundred years. Germany tried to commit a crime against civilization, and this Treaty is justified in making Germany pay for that criminal error up to the ability of her payment. It is a very severe settlement with Germany, but there is not anything in it she did not earn. Indeed, she earned more than she can ever be able to pay for, and the punishment exacted of her is not a punishment greater than she can bear, and it is absolutely necessary in order that no other nation may ever plot such a thing against humanity and civilization. It is a Treaty made by men who had no intention of crushing the German people, but who did mean to have it burnt into the consciousness of the German people, and through their consciousness into the apprehension of the world, that no people could afford to live under a government which was not controlled by their purpose and will and which was at liberty to impose secret ambitions upon the civilization of the world. It was intended as notice to all mankind that any government that attempted what Germany attempted would meet with the same just retribution. All that this Treaty amounts to, so far as Germany is concerned, is that she shall be obliged to pay every dollar that she can afford to pay to repair the damage that she did; except for territorial arrangements which it includes, that is practically the whole of the Treaty so far as concerns Germany. Germany's worst punishment is not in the Treaty, it is in her relations with the rest of mankind for the next generation.

No indemnity of any sort was claimed, merely reparation, merely paying for the destruction done, merely making good the losses so far as such losses could be made good which she had unjustly inflicted, not upon the Governments, for the reparation is not to go to the Governments, but upon the people whose rights she had trodden upon with absolute absence of everything that even resembled pity. Even in the terms of reparation a method is devised by which the reparations shall be adjusted to Germany's ability to pay it. There is a method of adjustment in that Treaty by which the reparation shall not be pressed beyond the point which Germany can pay, but which will be pressed to the utmost point that Germany can pay, which is just, which is righteous.

We tried to be just to Germany, and when we had heard her arguments and examined every portion of the counter proposals that she made, we wrote the Treaty in its final form and then said, "Sign here." What else did our boys die for? Did they die in order that we might ask Germany's leave to complete our victory? They died in order that we might say to Germany what the terms of victory were in the interest of justice and of peace, and we were entitled to take the course that we did take. It would have been intolerable if there had been anything else. What has not been borne in upon the consciousness of some of our people is that although most of the words of the Treaty are devoted to the settlement with Germany, the greater part of the meaning of its provisions is devoted to the settlement of the world.

It is a world settlement, the first ever attempted, attempted upon broad lines which were first laid down in America. You remember that we laid down Fourteen Points which should contain the principles of the settlement. They were not my points. In every one of them I was conscientiously trying to read the thought of the people of the United States, and after I uttered those points I had every assurance given me that could be given me that they did speak the moral judgment of the United States. Then when it came to that critical period, when it was evident that the war was coming to its critical end, all the nations engaged in the war accepted those fourteen principles explicitly as the basis of the armistice and the basis of the peace. All of Europe was aware that what was being done was building up an American peace. Every man who looks at it without party prejudice and as an American, will find in that Treaty more things that are genuinely American than were ever put into any similar document before.

One of the things that America has had most at heart throughout her existence has been that there should be substituted for the brutal processes of war the friendly processes of consultation and arbitration, and that is done in the Covenant of the League of Nations. Consultation, discussion, is written all over the face of the Covenant of the League of Nations, for the heart of it is that the nations promise not to go to war until they have consulted, until they have discussed, until all the facts in the controversy have been laid before the court which represents the common opinion of mankind. The League of Nations substitutes discussion for fight, and without discussion there will be fight. One of the greatest difficulties we have been through in the past is in getting men to understand that fundamental thing.

DISARMAMENT

And there was another thing that we wished to accomplish that is accomplished in this document. We wanted disarmament, and this document provides it in the only possible way for disarmament, by common agreement. Every great fighting nation in the world is to be a member of this partnership except Germany, and inasmuch as Germany has accepted a limitation of her army to 100,000 men, I can not think for the time being she may be regarded as a great fighting nation. Here in the center of Europe a great nation of more than 60,000,000 that has agreed not to maintain an army of more than 100,000 men, and all around her the rest of the world in concerted partnership to see that no other nation attempts what she attempted, and agreeing among themselves that they will not impose this limitation of armament upon Germany merely, but that they will impose it upon themselves. There is no other way to dispense with great armaments except by the common agreement of the fighting nations of the world; and here in the agreement. They promise disarmament and they promise to agree upon a plan.

INTERNATIONAL COURT

All the nations agree to join in devising a plan for general disarmament. You have heard that this Covenant was a plan for bringing on war. Well, it is going to bring on war by means of disarmament and also by establishing a permanent court of international justice. When I voted for that, I was obeying the mandate of the Congress of the United States. In a very unexpected place, namely, in a Naval Appropriation Bill, passed in 1915, it is declared to be the policy of the United States to bring about a general disarmament by common agreement, and the President of the United States was requested to call a conference not later than the close of the then present war for the purpose of consulting and agreeing upon a plan for a permanent court of international justice; and he was authorized in case such an agreement could be reached, to stop the building programme provided for by that Naval Appropriation Bill. The Congress of the United States deliberately not only accepted but directed the President to promote an agreement of this sort for disarmament and a permanent court of international justice. Not satisfied with putting it there once, they put it there several times; I mean in successive years. It even went so far as to make an appropriation to pay the expenses by a continuing provision in the Naval Appropriation Bill. They looked forward to it with such a practical eye that they contemplated the possibility of its coming soon enough to stop the building program of that bill.

You know what a permanent court of international justice implies. The difficulty which is being found with the League of Nations is that apparently the gentlemen who are discussing it unfavorably are afraid that we will be bound to do something we do not want to. The only way in which you can have impartial determinations in this world is by consenting to something you do not want to do. Every time you have a case in court one or other of the parties has to consent to do something he does not want to do. There is not a case in court, and there are hundreds of thousands of them every year, in which one of the parties is not disappointed. Yet we regard that as the foundation of civilization, that we will not fight about these things, and that when we lose in court we will take our medicine. Very well, I say the two Houses of Congress suggested that there be an international court and suggested that they were willing to take their medicine. You cannot set up a court without respecting its decrees. You cannot make a toy of it. You cannot make a mockery of it. If you, indeed, want a court, then you must abide by the judgments of the court; and we have declared already that we were willing to abide by the judgments of a court of international justice. If we are, indeed, headed toward peace with the real purpose of our hearts engaged, then we must take the necessary steps to secure it, and we must make the necessary sacrifices to secure it.

LAND TITLES OF EUROPE

One of the interesting things that this Treaty does is to settle the land titles of Europe, and to settle them in this way—on the principle that every land belongs to the people that live on it. This is actually the first time in human history that that principle was ever recognized in a similar document, and yet that is the fundamental American principle. The fundamental American principle is the right of the people that live in the country to say what shall be done with that country. We have gone so far in our assertions of popular right that we not only say that the people have a right to have a government that suits them, but that they have a right to change it in any respect at any time. That principle lies at the heart of this Treaty.

Wherever there was a doubtful district we applied the same principle, that the people should decide and not the men sitting around the peace table at Paris. It was not easy to draw the line. It was not a surveyor's task. There were not well known points from which to start and to which to go, because, for example, we were trying to give the Bohemians the lands where the Bohemians lived, but the Bohemians did not stop at a straight line. If they will pardon the expression, they slopped over. And Germans slopped over into Poland and in some cases there was an almost inextricable mixture of the two populations. Take what in Europe they call High Silesia, the mountainous, the upper portions of the District of Silesia. The very great majority of the people in High Silesia are Poles, but the Germans contested the statement that most of them were Poles. Everybody said that the statistics lied. They said the German statistics with regard to High Silesia, for example, were not true, because the Germans want to make it out that the Germans were in a majority there, and the Poles declared that the Poles were in a majority there. We said, "This is a difficult business. Sitting in Paris we cannot tell by count how many Poles there are in High Silesia, or how many Germans, and if we could count them, we cannot tell from Paris, what they want. High Silesia does not belong to us, it does not belong to anybody but the people who live in it. We will do this: We will put that territory under the care of the League of Nations for a little period; we will establish a small armed force there, made up of contingents out of the different allied nations so that no one of them would be in control, and then we will hold a referendum, and High Silesia shall belong either to Germany or to Poland as the people in High Silesia shall desire."

That is only one case out of half a dozen. In regions where the make up of the population is doubtful or the desire of the population is as yet unascertained, the League of Nations is to be the instrumentality by which the goods are to be delivered to the people to whom they belong. No other international conference ever conceived such a purpose and no earlier conference of that sort would have been willing to carry out such a purpose.

EUROPEAN WATERWAYS

The makers of the Treaty proceeded to arrange upon a cooperative basis those things which had always been arranged upon a competitive basis. I want to mention a very practical thing which most of you, I dare say, never thought about. Most of the rivers of Europe traverse the territory of several nations, and up to the time of this peace conference there had been certain historic rights and certain treaty rights over parts of the courses of those rivers which had embarrassed the people who lived higher up upon the stream; just as if the great Mississippi, for example, passed through half a dozen states and the people down at New Orleans lived under a government which could control the navigation of the lower parts of the Mississippi. There were abundant instances of that sort in Europe, and this Treaty undertakes to internationalize all the great waterways of that continent, to see to it that their several portions are taken out of national control and put under international control, so that the stream that passes through one nation shall be just as free in all its length to the sea as if that nation owned the whole of it, and nobody shall have the right to put a restriction upon their passage to the sea. I mention this in order to illustrate the heart of this Treaty, which is to cut out national privilege and give to every people the full right attaching to the territory in which they live. The Treaty does not stop there. It attempts to coordinate all the great humane endeavors of the world. It tries to bring under international cooperation every effort to check international crime. I mean like that unspeakable traffic in women, like that almost equally unspeakable traffic in children. It undertakes a new method of cooperation among all the great Red Cross societies of the world. I say without hesitation that no international agreement has ever before been drawn up along those lines, of universal consideration of right and the interest of humanity—and I have not half described the Treaty.

MAGNA CHARTA OF LABOR

You have heard of the Covenant of the League of Nations until, I dare say, you suppose that is the only thing in the Treaty. On the contrary, there is a document almost as extensive in the latter part of the treaty which is nothing less than a great charter of liberty for the working men and women of the world. This Treaty contains the organization by which the united counsels of mankind shall attempt to lift the levels of labor and see that men who are working with their hands are everywhere treated as they ought to be treated, upon principles of justice and equality. How many laboring men dreamed, when this war began, that four years later it would be possible for all the great nations of the world to enter into a covenant like that?

One of the most striking and useful provisions of the Treaty is that every member of the League of Nations undertakes to advance the humane conditions of labor for men, women and children, to consider the interests of labor under its own jurisdiction and to try to extend to every nation with which it has any dealings, the standards of labor upon which it itself insists; so that America, which has by no means yet reached the standards in these matters which we must and shall reach, but which nevertheless, is the most advanced in the world in respect of the conditions of labor, undertakes to bring all the influence it can legitimately bear upon every nation with which it has any dealings to see that labor there is put upon as good a footing as labor in America. Perhaps some of you have not kept in mind the Seamen's Act which was passed in a recent session of Congress. Under the law before that Act, seamen could be bound to the service of their ship in such fashion that when they came to the ports of the United States, if they tried to leave their ship, the Government of the United States was bound to arrest them and send them back to their ship. The Seamen's Act abrogates that law and practically makes it necessary for every ship that would take away from the United States the crew that it brings to it, shall pay American wages to get it. I hear very little said about this Magna Charta of labor which is embodied in this Treaty. It forecasts the day which ought to have come long ago, when statesmen will realize that no nation is fortunate which is not happy, and that no nation can be happy whose people are not contented—contented in their lives and fortunate in the circumstances of their lives.

The cost of living at present is a world condition. The high cost of living is one of those things which are so complicated; it ramifies in so many directions that it seems to me we can not do anything in particular without knowing how the particulars affect the whole. Until the industrial world here and elsewhere is put on its feet you cannot finally handle the question of the cost of living because the cost of living in the last analysis depends upon the things we are always talking about but do not know how to manage—the law of supply and demand. It depends upon manufacture and distribution. It depends upon all the normal processes of the industrial and commercial world. It depends upon international credit. It depends upon shipping. It depends upon the multiplication of transportation facilities domestically. Our railroads at this moment are not adequate to moving the commerce of this country. Terminal facilities at the ports are not adequate. The problem grows the more you think of it. What we have to put our minds to is an international problem, first of all—to set the commerce of the world going again and the manufacture of the world going again. And we have got to do that largely. Then we have got to see that our own production and our own methods of finance and our own commerce are quickened in every way that is possible.

Not only that but we have got to realize that we are face to face with a great industrial problem which does not center in the United States. It centers elsewhere, but which we share with the other countries of the world. That is the relation between capital and labor, between those who employ and those who are employed. All through the world the one central question of civilization is, "What shall be the conditions of labor?" Why is it that labor organizations jealously limit the amount of work that their men can do? Because they are driving hard bargains with you; they do not feel that they are your partners at all, and so long as labor and capital are antagonistic production is going to be at its minimum. Just so soon as they are sympathetic and cooperative it is going to abound, and that will be one of the means of bringing down the cost of living. The laboring men of the world are not satisfied with their relations with their employers. Of course, I do not mean to say that there is universal dissatisfaction, because here, there and elsewhere, in many cases fortunately, there are very satisfactory relations, but I am now speaking of the general relationship which exists between capital and labor.

What the world now insists upon is the establishment of industrial democracy. There must be a reconsideration of the structure of our economic society. There are all sorts of readjustments necessary in this country. There must be some very fundamental economic reforms in this country. We have got to have a constructive program with regard to labor, and the minute we get it we will relieve the strain all over the world, because the world will accept our standards and follow our example. I cannot presume that I know how it ought to be done. I know the principle. The principle is that the interest of capital and the interest of labor are not different but the same, and men of business sense ought to know how to work out an organization which will express that identity of interest. Where there is identity of interest there must be community of interest. You cannot longer regard labor as a commodity. You have got to regard it as a means of association, the association of physical skill and physical vigor with the enterprise which is managed by those who represent capital; and when you do, the production of the world is going to go forward by leaps and bounds. If you want to realize the real wealth of this country, then bring about the human relationship between employers and employees which will make them colaborers and partners and fellow workers. The point I wish to make is that the world is looking to America to set the standards with regard to the conditions of labor and the relations between labor and capital, and looking to us because we have been more progressive than other nations in those matters, though sometimes we have moved very slowly and with undue caution. As a result of our progressiveness the ruling influences among our working men are conservative in the sense that they see that it is not in the interest of labor to break up civilization, and progressive in the sense that they see that a constructive program has to be adopted. We must devote our national genius to working out a method of association between the two which will make this Nation the nation to solve triumphantly and for all time the fundamental problem of peaceful production.

You ask, "What has that got to do with the League of Nations?" I dare say you do not know because I have never heard anyone tell you that the great charter, the new constitutional charter of labor is in the Treaty of peace and associated with the League of Nations. A great machinery of consultation is set up there, not merely about international political affairs, but about standards of labor, about the relationships between managers and employees, about the labor of women and of children, about the humane side and the business side of the whole labor problem.

NO NATIONAL TRIUMPHS

There is no national triumph sought to be recorded in this Treaty. The chief thing to notice about it is that it is the first Treaty ever made by the great powers that was not made in their own favor. There is no glory sought for any particular nation. The fundamental principle of this Treaty is a principle never acknowledged before, a principle which had its birth and has had its growth in this country, that the countries of the world belong to the people who live in them, and that they have a right to determine their own destiny and their own form of government, and their own policy, and that no body of statesmen, sitting anywhere, no matter whether they represented the overwhelming physical force of the world or not, has the right to assign any great people to a sovereignty under which it does not care to live. For the first time in the history of civilized society, a great international convention, made up of the leading statesmen of the world, has proposed a settlement which is for the benefit of the weak and not for the benefit of the strong. It is for the benefit of peoples who could not have liberated themselves, whose weakness was profitable to the ambitious and imperialistic nations, whose weakness had been traded in by every cabinet in Europe; and yet these very cabinets represented at the table in Paris, were unanimous in the conviction that the peoples' day had come and that it was not their right to dispose of the fortunes of people without the consent of these people themselves.

This Treaty is an attempt to right the history of Europe. The heart of this Treaty is not that it punishes Germany—that is a temporary thing—it is that it rectifies the age-long wrongs which characterized the history of Europe. This is a Treaty not merely for the nations represented at the peace table but for the people who were the subjects of governments whose wrongs were righted on the fields of France. Insofar as the scope of our authority went, we rectified the wrongs which have been the fertile source of war in Europe.

NO ANNEXATIONS

There is not a single act of annexation in this Treaty. Every other international arrangement had been a division of spoils, and this is an absolute renunciation of spoils. Even the territories that are taken away from Germany, like her colonies, are not given to anybody.

When we turned to the property of Germany, which she had been habitually misgoverning—I mean the German colonies, particularly the colonies in Africa—there were many nations who would like to have had those rich, undeveloped portions of the world; but none of them got them. We adopted the principle of trusteeship. We said, "We will put you in charge of this, that, and the other piece of territory, and you will make an annual report to us. We will deprive you of your trusteeship whenever you administer it in a way which is not approved by our judgment, and we will put upon you this primary limitation, that you shall do nothing that is to the detriment of the people who live in that territory. You shall not enforce labor on it, and you shall apply the same principles of humanity to the work of their women and children that you apply at home. You shall not allow men who want to make money out of powder and shot to sell arms and ammunition to those men who can use them to their own disadvantage. You shall not make those people fight in your armies. The country is theirs, and you must remember that and treat it as theirs.

There is no more annexation. There is no more land grabbing. There is no more extension of sovereignty. We have put the same safeguards, and as adequate safeguards, around the poor naked fellows in the jungles of Africa that we have around those poor peoples almost ready to assume the full rights of self government in some parts of the Turkish Empire: for example Armenia. Armenia is one of the regions that are to be under trust of the League of Nations. Armenia is to be redeemed. The Turk is to be forbidden to exercise authority there, and the Christian people are not only to be allowed to aid Armenia but they are to be allowed to protect Armenia. At last this great people, struggling through night after night of terror, knowing not what day would see their land stained with blood, are now given a promise of safety, a promise of justice, and a possibility that they may come out into a time when they can enjoy their own rights as free people, as they never dreamed they would be able to exercise them before. The principle is adopted without qualification upon which America was founded that all just government proceeds from the consent of the governed.

This Treaty is a readjustment of all those great injustices that underlie the whole structure of European and Asiatic society. Matters are drawn into this Treaty which affected the peace and happiness of the whole continent of

Europe, and not of the continent of Europe merely, but of forlorn populations in Africa, of peoples that we hardly know about in Asia, in the Far East, and everywhere the influences of German policy extended and everywhere that influence had to be corrected, had to be checked, had to be altered. The heart of the Treaty is that it undoes the injustice that Germany did; that it not only undoes the injustice that Germany did but it organizes the world to see that such injustice will in the future be impossible.

When you look at the Treaty of Peace with Germany in the light of what I have been saying to you, everything else is put in a different light. It is the chart and constitution of a new system for the world, and that new system is based upon an absolute reversal of the principles of the old system. This Treaty contains the things that America believes in. This is one of the great charters of human liberty, and the man who picks flaws in it, or, rather, picks out the flaws that are in it, for there are flaws in it, forgets the magnitude of the thing, forgets the majesty of the thing, forgets that the councils of more than twenty nations combined and were rendered unanimous in the adoption of this great instrument. This settlement is the first international settlement that was intended for the happiness of the average men and women throughout the world.

America in this Treaty has realized what those gallant boys we are so proud of fought for. Do not let your thoughts dwell too constantly upon Germany. Germany attempted this outrageous thing, but Germany was not the only country that had ever entertained the purpose of subjecting the peoples of the world to its will, and when we went into this war we said that we sent our soldiers across the seas not because we thought this was an American fight in particular, but because we knew that the purpose of Germany was against liberty, and that where anybody was fighting liberty it was our duty to go into the contest. We set this Nation up with the profession that we wanted to set an example of liberty not only, but to lead the world in the paths of liberty and justice and of right; and at last, after long reflection, after long hesitation, after trying to persuade ourselves that this was a European war and nothing more, we suddenly looked our own conscience in the face and said, "This is not merely a European war. This is a war which imperils the very principles for which this Government was set up, and it is our duty to lend all the force that we have, whether of men or of resources, to the resistance of these designs." And it was America—never let anybody forget this—it was America that saved the world, and those who propose the rejection of the Treaty propose that, after having redeemed the world, we should desert the world. It would be nothing less.

After all the rest of the world has signed it, gentlemen will find it very difficult to make any other kind of Treaty. You cannot have any other treaty, because you can never get together again the elements that agreed to this Treaty. The rejection of this Treaty means the necessity of negotiating a separate treaty with Germany. A separate peace with the Central Powers could accomplish nothing but our eternal disgrace! That separate treaty between Germany and the United States could not alter any sentence in this Treaty. It could not affect the validity of any sentence in this Treaty. You cannot assemble the forces again that were back of it. You cannot do it by dealing with separate governments. You cannot bring the agreement upon which it rests into force again. It was the laborious work of many, many months of the most intimate conference. It has very, very few compromises in it, and is, most of it, laid down in straight lines according to American specifications. I hope that in order to strengthen this impression on your minds that you will take the

pains to read the Treaty of peace. A good deal
of it is technical and you could skip that part,
but read all of it that you do not need an expert to advise you with regard to the meaning
of. The economic and financial clauses which
particularly affect the settlements with Germany are, I dare say, almost unintelligible to
most people, but you do not have to understand them; they are going to be worked out
by experts. The rest of it is going to be worked
out by the experience of free self-governed
peoples. I wish you would get a copy of it and
read it. If you will not take the pains to do
that, you will accept the interpretation of
those who made it and know what the inten-
tions were in the making of it.

AMERICAN EXPERTS

At the peace table one of the reasons why
American advice continually prevailed, as it
did, was that our experts, our financial experts, our economic experts, and all the rest of
us—for you must remember that the work of
the conference was not done exclusively by the
men whose names you all read about every
day; it was done by the most intensive labor
of experts of every sort who sat down together
and got down to the hardpan of every subject
that they had to deal with—were known to be
disinterested, and in nine cases out of ten,

after a long series of debates and interchanges of views and counter-proposals, it was usually the American proposal that was adopted. That was because the American experts came at last into this position of advantage, they had convinced everybody that they were not trying to work anything, that they were not thinking of something that they did not disclose, that they wanted all the cards on the table, and that they wanted to deal with nothing but facts. They were not dealing with national ambitions, they were not trying to disappoint anybody, and they were not trying to stack the cards for anybody. It was that conviction, and that only, which led to the success of American counsel in Paris.[1] Is not that a worthy heritage for people who set up a great free Nation on this continent in order to lead men in the ways of justice and of liberty!

I think I can take it for granted that you never realized before what a scope this great Treaty has. You have been asked to look at so many little spots in it with a magnifying glass that you did not know how big it is, what a great enterprise of the human spirit it is, and what a thoroughly American document it is from cover to cover. It is astonishing that this great document did not come as a shock upon

[1]See Appendix C.

the world. If the world had not already been rent by the great struggle which preceded this settlement, men would have stood at amaze at such a document as this. It is the most remarkable document, I venture to say, in human history, because in it is recorded a complete reversal of the processes of government which had gone on throughout practically the whole history of mankind. The example that we set in 1776, which some statesmen in Europe affected to disregard and others presumed to ridicule, nevertheless set fires going in the hearts of men which no influence was able to quench, and one after another the governments of the world have yielded to the influences of Democracy. And there came a day at Paris when the representatives of all the great Governments of the world accepted the American specifications upon which the terms of the Treaty of Peace were drawn.

The choice is either to accept this Treaty or to play a lone hand. What does that mean? That means that we must always be armed, that we must always be ready to mobilize the man strength and the manufacturing resources of the country; it means that we must continue to live under not diminishing but increasing taxes; it means that we shall develop our thought and the organization of our Government to being strong enough to beat any nation in the world. An absolute reversal of all the ideals of American history.

If you are going to play a lone hand, the hand that you play must be upon the handle of the sword. You cannot play a lone hand and do your civil business except with the other hand—one hand incidental for the business of peace, and the other hand constantly for the assertion of force. It is either this Treaty or a lone hand, and the lone hand must have a weapon in it. The weapon must be all the young men of the country trained to arms, and the business of the country must pay the piper, must pay for the whole armament, the arms and the men.

In the debate of this great document, I think, a great many things that we talked about at first have cleared away. A great many difficulties which were at first discovered, or which some fancied that they had discovered, have been removed. The center and heart of this document is that great instrument which is placed at the beginning of it, the Covenant of the League of Nations. I think everybody now understands that you cannot work this Treaty without that Covenant. Everybody certainly understands that you have no insurance for the continuance of this settlement without the Covenant of the League of Nations, and you will notice that, with the single exception of the provision with regard to the transfer of the German rights in Shantung in China to Japan, practically nothing in the body of the Treaty has seemed to constitute any great obstacle to its adoption. All the controversy, all the talk, has centered on the League of Nations, and I am glad to see the issue center; I am glad to see the issue clearly drawn, for now we have to decide. Shall we stand by the settlements of liberty or shall we not? The representatives of all the great Governments of the world accepted the American specifications upon which the terms of the Treaty of Peace were drawn. In order to carry this Treaty out, it is necessary to reconstruct Europe economically and industrially. If we do not take part in that reconstruction, we will be shut out from it, and by consequence the markets of Europe will be shut to us. The combinations of European governments can be formed to exclude us wherever it is possible to exclude us; and if you want to come to the hard and ugly basis of material interest, the United States will everywhere trade at an overwhelming disadvantage just as soon as we have forfeited, and deserve to forfeit, the confidence of the world. Shall we keep the primacy of the world, or shall we abandon it? Shall we have our Treaty, or shall we have somebody else's? It is an absolute reversal of history, an absolute revolution in the way in which international affairs are treated, and it is all in the Covenant of the League of Nations.

THE LEAGUE OF NATIONS

WE have shown Germany—and not Germany only, but the world—that upon occasion the great peoples of the world will combine to prevent an iniquity, but we have not shown how that is going to be done in the future with a certainty that will make every other nation know that a similar enterprise must not be attempted.

That is what the League of Nations is for—to end this war justly and then not merely to serve notice on governments which would contemplate the same things that Germany contemplated that they will do it at their peril, but also concerning the combination of power which will prove to them they will do it at their peril. It is idle to say the world will combine against you, because it may not, but it is persuasive to say the world is combined against you and will remain combined against the things that Germany attempted.

I want, by way of introduction and clarification, to point out what is not often enough explained in this country—the actual constitution of the League of Nations.

If you will be generous enough to read some of the things I say, I hope it will clarify a great many matters which have been very much obscured by some of the things which have been said.

I want to contrast some things that have been said with the real facts.

I want to give you a very simple account of the organization of the League of Nations and let you judge for yourselves.

It is very simply constituted—it consists of two bodies, a Council and an Assembly.

THE COUNCIL

There is the Council, which consists of one representative from each of the principal allied and associated powers, that is to say, the United States, Great Britain, France, Italy and Japan, along with four representatives of smaller powers chosen out of the general body of the membership of the League.[1]

The whole direction of the action of the League is vested in the Council. The Council is the only part of the organization that can take effective action. Nothing in the form of an active measure, no policy, no recommendation with regard to the action of the governments composing the League can proceed except upon a unanimous vote of the Council. Mark you, a unanimous vote of the Council.

[1] This number at the request of the Council, has now been increased to six smaller powers, Belgium, Brazil, China, Spain, Sweden and Uruguay.

That is explicitly stated in the Covenant itself. Does it not evidently follow that the League of Nations can adopt no policy whatever, without the consent of the United States? In brief, inasmuch as the United States is to be a permanent member of the Council of the League, the League can take no step whatever without the consent of the United States of America. We are so safeguarded that the world under the Covenant cannot do a thing that we do not consent to being done. There is not a single active step that the League can take unless we vote aye. Think of the significance of that!

THE ASSEMBLY

The Assembly is a debating body. The Assembly is the numerous body. In it every self-governing State that is a member of the League is represented, and not only the self-governing, independent States, but the self-governing colonies and dominions, such as Canada, New Zealand, Australia, India and South Africa. Each member of the Assembly has three representatives.

The Assembly is, so to say, the court of the public opinion of the world. It is where you can debate anything that affects the peace of the world, but not determine upon a course of action upon anything that affects the peace of the world. The Assembly is the talking body. The Assembly was created in order that anybody that purposed anything wrong should be subjected to the awkward circumstance that everybody could talk about it. This is the great assembly in which all the things that are likely to disturb the peace of the world or the good understanding between nations are to be exposed to the general view. The voice of the world is at last released. The conscience of the world is at last given a forum, and the rights of men not liberated under this Treaty are given a place where they can be heard. If there are nations which wish to exercise the power of self-determination but are not liberated by this Treaty, they can come into that great forum, they can point out how their demands affect the peace and quiet of the world, they can point out how their demands affect the good understanding between nations.

There is a forum here for the rights of mankind which was never dreamed of before, and in that forum any representative has the right to speak his full mind. Never before has this been possible. Never before has there been a jury of mankind to which nations could take their causes, whether they were weak or strong. I am amazed that so many men do not see the extraordinary change which this will bring in the transaction of human affairs. I am amazed that they do not see that now, for the first time, not selfish national policy but the general judgment of the world as to right is going to determine the fortunes of peoples, whether they be weak or whether they be strong.

The Assembly is not a voting body, except upon a limited number of questions, and whenever those questions are questions of action, the affirmative vote of every nation represented on the Council is indispensable. In every matter in which the Assembly can vote along with the Council it is necessary that all the nations represented on the Council should concur in the affirmative vote to make it valid, so that in every vote, no matter how many concur in it in the Assembly, in order for it to become valid, it is necessary that the United States should vote aye. There is a very limited number of subjects upon which it can act at all, and I have taken the pains to write them down here, after again and again going through the Covenant for the purpose of making sure that I had not omitted anything, in order that I might give you an explicit account of the thing. There are two matters in which the Assembly can act, but I do not think we will be jealous of them. A majority of the Assembly can advise a member of the

League to reconsider any treaty which, in the opinion of the Assembly of the League, is apt to conflict with the operation of the League itself, but that is advice which can be disregarded, which has no validity of action in it, which has no compulsion of law in it. There is one matter upon which the Assembly can vote, and which it can decide by a two-thirds majority without the concurrence of all the States represented in the council, and that is the admission of new members to the League.

There are two things which a majority of the Assembly may do. Here are the cases. When the Council refers a matter in dispute to the Assembly, the Assembly can decide by a majority, provided all the representatives of the nations represented in the Council vote on the side of the majority. In case of an amendment to the Covenant it is necessary that there should be a unanimous vote of the representatives of the nations which are represented in the Council in addition to a majority vote of the Assembly itself. In the Assembly as in the Council, any single nation that is a member of the Council has a veto upon active conclusions, and there is all the voting that the Assembly does.

Everything that is done by the League is formulated and passed by the Council and a unanimous vote is required. I share with all my fellow countrymen a very great jealousy with regard to setting up any power that could tell us to do anything but no such power is set up. All the action, all the energy, all the initiative of the League of Nations is resident in the Council, and in the Council a unanimous vote is necessary for action, and no action is possible without the concurrent vote of the United States. I cannot understand why, having read the Covenant of the League and examined its constitution, they are not satisfied with the fact that every active policy of the League must be concurred in by a unanimous vote of the Council, which means that the affirmative vote of the United States is in every instance necessary.

That is the only thing that seems to me weak about the League, I am afraid that a unanimous vote will sometimes be very difficult to get. The danger is not action, but inaction. The danger is not that they will do something that we do not like, but that upon some critical occasion they will not do anything. That may sometimes, I am afraid, impede the action of the League; but at any rate, it makes the sovereignty and the sovereign choice of every nation that is a member of the League absolutely safe. Every other government, big or little, or middle-sized, that had to be dealt with in Paris, was just as jealous of its sovereignty as the United States. The only difference between some of them and us is that we can take care of our own sovereignty and they could not take care of theirs, but it has been a matter of principle with the United States to maintain that in respect of rights there was and should be no difference between a weak state and a strong state. Our contention has always been in international affairs, that we should deal with them upon the absolute equality of independent sovereignty, and that is the organization of the League.

ONLY FREE GOVERNMENTS ADMITTED

Only the free peoples of the world can join the League of Nations. No nation is admitted to the League of Nations that cannot show that it has the institutions which we call free. No autocratic government can come into its membership, no government which is not controlled by the will and vote of its people. Nobody is admitted except the self-governing nations, because it was the instinctive judgment of every man who sat around that board that only a nation whose government was its servant and not its master could be trusted to preserve the peace of the world. It is a league of free independent peoples all over the world and when that great arrangement is consummated there is not going to be a ruler in the world that does not take his advice from his people. There are not going to be many other kinds of nations long. The people of this world—not merely the people of America, for they did the job long ago—have determined that there shall be no more autocratic governments. The Hapsburgs and the Hohenzollerns are permanently out of business. They are out of date because this Great War with its triumphal issue, marks a new day in the history of the world.

MAINTENANCE OF WORLD PEACE

The Covenant of the League of Nations is the instrumentality for the maintenance of peace. How does it propose to maintain it? At the heart of that Covenant there are these tremendous arrangements—every member of the League solemnly agrees, that means all the nations of the world, great and small, that means every fighting nation in the world, because for the present, limited to an army of 100,000, Germany is not a fighting nation—that it will never go to war without first having done one or another of two things: without either submitting the matter in dispute to arbitration, in which case it promises absolutely to abide by the verdict, or, if it does not care to submit it to arbitration, without submitting it to discussion by the council of the League of Nations, in which case it promises to lay all the documents and all the pertinent facts before that Council; it consents that that Council shall publish all the documents and all the pertinent facts, so that all the world shall know them; that it shall be allowed six months in which to consider the matter; and that even at the end of six months, if the decision of the Council is not acceptable, it will not go to war for three months following the rendering of the decision. So that, even allowing no time for preliminaries, there are nine months of cooling off, nine months of discussion, nine months not of private discussion, not of discussion between those who are heated, but of discussion between those who are disinterested except in the maintenance of the peace of the world when the influence of the public opinion of mankind is brought to bear upon the contest. That is the central principle of some thirty treaties entered into between the United States of America and some thirty other sovereign nations, all of which were confirmed by the Senate of the United States. Any nation that is in the wrong and waits nine months before it goes to war will never go to war. No nation is going to look the calm judgment of mankind in the face for nine months and then go to war! If anything approaching that had been the arrangement of the world in 1914, the war would have been impossible; and I confidently predict that there is not an aggressive people in the world who would dare bring a wrongful purpose to that jury. It is the most formidable jury in the world. It is not only a union of free peoples to guarantee civilization; it is something more than that. It is a League of Nations to advance civilization by substituting something that will make the improvement of civilization possible.

BOYCOTT

If any member of the League breaks or ignores these promises with regard to arbitration and discussion, what happens? War? No, not war but something that will interest them and engage them very much more than war, something more tremendous than war. All the arguments you hear are based upon the assumption that we are all going to break the Covenant; that bad faith is the accepted rule. I repudiate the suggestion which underlies some of the suggestions I have heard that the other nations of the world are acting in bad faith and that only the United States is acting in good faith. It is not true! I can testify that I was cooperating with honorable men on the other side of the water, and I challenge anybody to show where in recent years, while the opinion of mankind has been effective, there has been the repudiation of an international obligation by France, or Italy, or Great Britain or by Japan.

I was glad after I inaugurated it that I drew together the little body which was called "the big four." We did not call it the "Big Four"; we called it something very much bigger than that. We called it the Supreme Council of the Principal and Allied and Associated Powers. We had to have some name and the more dramatic it was the better; but it was a very simple council of friends. The intimacies of that little room were the center of the whole Peace Cconference, and they were the intimacies of men who believed in the same things and sought the same objects. The hearts of men like Clemenceau and Lloyd-George and Orlando beat with the people of the world as well as with the people of their own countries. They have the same fundamental sympathies that we have and they know that there is only one way to work out peace and that is to work it out right. There has not been any such bad faith among nations in recent times except the flagrant bad faith of the nation we have just been fighting, and that bad faith is not likely to be repeated in the immediate future.

Suppose somebody does not abide by those

engagements, then what happens? An absolute isolation, a boycott! The boycott is automatic. There is no "if" or "but" about that in the Covenant. It is provided in the Covenant that any nation that disregards these solemn promises with regard to arbitration and discussion shall be thereby deemed "ipso facto" to have committed an act of war against the other members of the League, and that there shall thereupon follow an absolute exclusion of that nation from communication of any kind with the members of the League. When you consider that the League is going to consist of every considerable nation in the world, except Germany—you can see what the boycott will mean. No goods can be shipped in or out, no telegraphic messages can be exchanged, except through the elusive wireless perhaps; there shall be no communication of any kind between the people of the other nations and the people of that nation. The nationals, the citizens of the member states will never enter their territory, until the matter is adjusted, and their citizens cannot leave their territory. It is the most complete boycott ever conceived in a public document; and I want to say with confident prediction that there will be no more fighting after that. There is not a nation that can stand that for six months. Germany could have faced the armies of the world more readily than she faced the boycott of the world. Germany felt the pinch of the blockade more than she felt the stress of the blow; and there is not, so far as I know, a single European country—I say European, because I think our own country is an exception—which is not dependent upon some other part of the world for some of the necessaries of its life. There is not a nation in Europe that can live for six months without importing goods out of other countries. Some of them are absolutely dependent, some are without the raw materials practically of any kind, some of them are absolutely without fuel of any kind, either coal or oil; almost all of them are without that variety of supply of ores which are necessary to modern industry and necessary to the manufacture of munitions of war.

I want you to realize that this war was won not only by the armies of the world. It was won by economic means as well. Without the economic means the war would have been much longer continued. What happened was that Germany was shut off from the economic resources of the globe and she could not stand it. What brought Germany to her knees was not only the splendid fighting of the incomparable men who met her armies, but it was that her doors were locked and she could not get supplies from any part of the world. There were a few doors open, to some Swedish ore for example, that she needed for making munitions, and that kept her going for a time, but the Swedish door would be shut this time. There would not be any door open; and that brings a nation to its senses just as suffocation removes from the individual all inclinations to fight. A nation that is boycotted is a nation that is in sight of surrender. Apply this economic, peaceful, silent, deadly remedy and there will be no need for force. It is a terrible remedy. It does not cost a life outside of the nation boycotted, but it brings a pressure upon that nation which, in my judgment, no modern nation could resist.

If this economic boycott bears with unequal weight the members of the League agree to support one another and to relieve one another in any exceptional disadvantages that may arise out of it. When you apply that boycott, you have got your hand upon the throat of the offending nation, and it is a proper punishment. It is an exclusion from civilized society. That is the remedy that thoughtful men have advocated for several generations. They have thought, and thought truly, that war was barbarous and that a nation that resorted to war when its cause was unjust was unworthy of being consorted with by free people anywhere.

The boycott is an infinitely more terrible instrument of war. The minute you lock the door, then the pinch of the thing becomes intolerable; not only the physical pinch, not only the fact that you cannot get raw materials and must stop your factories, not only the fact that you cannot get credit is stopped, that your assets are useless, but the still greater pinch that comes when a nation knows that it is sent to coventry and despised. To be put in jail is not the most terrible punishment that happens to a condemned man; if he knows that he was justly condemned, what penetrates his heart is the look in other men's eyes. It is the soul that is wounded much more poignantly than the body, and one of the things that the German nation has not been able to comprehend is that it has lost for the time being, the respect of mankind; and as Germans, when the doors of truth were opened to them after the war, have begun to realize that, they have begun to look aghast at the probable fortunes of Germany, for if the world does not trust them, if the world does not respect them, if the world does not want Germans to come as immigrants any more, what is Germany to do? The boycott is what is substituted for war.

THE LEAGUE OF NATIONS

Your attention is called to certain features of this League. I want to discuss with you very frankly, indeed just as frankly as I know how, the difficulties that have been suggested, to analyze the objections which are made to this great League. You have heard, I dare say, only about four things in the Covenant of the League of Nations, the chance to get out, the dangers of Article Ten, the Monroe Doctrine and the risk that other nations may interfere in our domestic affairs. I want very briefly to take these things in their sequence.

When this Covenant was drawn up in its first form, I had occasion to return to this country for a week or so. I brought the Covenant in its first draft. I then invited the Foreign Affairs Committee of the House, and the Foreign Relations Committee of the Senate to the White House to dinner, and after dinner we had the frankest possible conference with regard to this draft, of every portion that they wished to discuss. They made certain specific suggestions as to what should be contained in this document when it was revised. When I went back to Paris I carried every suggestion that was made in that conference to the commission on the League of Nations, which consisted of representatives of

[73]

other condition? Would you wish the United States allowed to withdraw without fulfilling its obligations? Is that the kind of people we are? The only thing that can ever keep you in the League is being ashamed to get out. You can get out whenever you want to after two years' notice and the only risk you run is having the rest of the world think you ought not to have gotten out. In as much as we have always scrupulously satisfied the public opinion of mankind with regard to justice and right I for my part, am not afraid at any time to go before that jury. It is a jury that might condemn us if we did wrong, but it is not a jury that could oblige us to stay in the League, so there is absolutely no limitation upon our right to withdraw.

ARTICLE TEN

Then comes Article Ten, for I am taking the questions in the order in which they come in the Covenant itself.

Article Ten is an engagement of the most extraordinary kind in history. It is an engagement by all the fighting nations of the world never to fight upon the plan upon which they always fought before.

There is nothing in Article Ten that can oblige the Congress of the United States to declare war if it does not deem it wise to declare war—and in case Congress is right I am indifferent to foreign opinion.

There is, however, something in Article Ten that you ought to realize and ought to accept or reject. Anybody who proposes to cut out Article Ten, proposes to cut out all the supports from under the peace and security of the world, and we must face the question in that light; we must draw the issue as sharply as that; we must see it through as distinctly as that. Article Ten, whether you want to assume the responsibility of it or not, is the heart of the pledge that we have made to the other nations of the world. Article Ten is the article that goes to the heart of this whole bad business, for that article says that the members of the League—that is intended to be all the great nations of the world—engage to respect and to preserve against all external aggression the territorial integrity and political independence of the nations concerned.

We are partners with the rest of the world in respecting the territorial integrity and political independence of others. Only by that article can we be said to have underwritten civilization. America alone cannot underwrite civilization. All the great free peoples of the world must underwrite it. We engage in the first sentence of Article Ten to respect and preserve from external aggression the territorial integrity and the existing political independence not only of the other states, but of all states, and if any member of the League disregards that promise, what happens? The second sentence provides that in case of necessity the council of the League shall advise what steps are necessary to carry out the obligations of that promise; that is to say, what force is necessary if any. The second sentence of Article Ten is that the Council shall advise as to the method of fulfilling this guarantee, that the Council which must vote by unanimous vote, must advise—cannot direct— what is to be done for the maintenance of the honor of its members and for the maintenance of the peace of the world. Is there anything that can frighten a man or a woman or a child with just thought or red blood, in those provisions?

Do you think the United States is likely to seize somebody else's territory? Do you think the United States is likely to disregard the first sentence of the article? The Council of the League advises what should be done to enforce the respect for that Covenant on the part of the nation attempting to violate it. It shall be the duty of the Council to advise, not to direct. Some gentlemen who doubt the meaning of English words have thought that advice did not mean advice but I do not know anything else that it does mean. I have in vain searched the dictionary to find any other meaning for the word "advise" than "advise." I can testify from having sat at the board where the instrument was drawn that advice means advice. You would think from some of the discussions that the emphasis is on the word "preserve." The solemn thing about Article Ten is the first sentence, not the second.

By guaranteeing the territorial integrity of a country you do not mean that you guarantee it against invasion. You guarantee it against the invader staying there and keeping the spoils. Territorial integrity does not mean that you cannot invade another country; it means that you cannot invade it and stay there. I have not impaired the territorial integrity of your back yard if I walk into it, but I very much impair it if I insist upon staying there and will not get out, and the impairment of integrity contemplated in this article is the kind of impairment as the seizure of territory, as an attempt at annexation, as an attempt at continuing domination either of the territory itself or of the methods of government inside that territory.

This does not guarantee any country, any government against an attempt on the part of its subjects to throw off its authority. It does not stop the right of revolution. It does not stop the choice of self-determination. No nation promises to protect any government against the wishes and actions of its own peoples or of any portion of its own people. The United States could not keep its countenance and make a promise like that, because it began by doing that very thing. She threw off the yoke of a government. Shall we prevent other people from throwing off the yoke that they are unwilling to bear? The glory of the United States is that when we were a little body of 3,000,000 people strung along the Atlantic coast we threw off the power of a great empire because it was not a power chosen by or consented to by ourselves. We hold that principle. We never will guarantee any government against the exercise of that right, and no suggestion was made in the conference that we should. We merely ourselves promised to respect the territorial integrity and existing political independence of the other members of the League and to assist in preserving them against external aggression.

Do not let anybody persuade you that you can take that article out and have a peaceful world. That promise is necessary in order to prevent this sort of war from recurring, and we are absolutely discredited if we fought this war and then neglect the essential safeguards against it. All the great wrongs of the world have had their root in the seizure of territory or the control of the political independence of other peoples. Without that clause the heart of the recent war is not cut out. The heart of the recent war was an absolute disregard of the territorial integrity and political independence of the smaller nations. If you do not cut the heart of the war out, that heart is going to live and beat and grow stronger and we will have the cataclysm again. That cuts at the root of the outrage against Belgium. That cuts at the root of the outrage against France. Article Ten cuts at the very heart, and is the only instrument that will cut at the very heart, of the old system.

For every other nation than Germany, in 1914, treaties stood as solemn and respected covenants. For Germany they were scraps of paper, and when her first soldier's foot fell upon the soil of Belgium her honor was forfeited. That act of aggression, that failure to respect the territorial integrity of a nation whose territory she was specially bound to respect, pointed the hand along that road that is strewn with graves since the beginning of history, that road made red and ugly with the strife behind which lies a disregard for the rights of others and a thought concentrated upon what you want and mean to get. That is the heart of war, and unless you accept Article Ten you do not cut the heart of war out of civilization. Article Ten is the test of the honor and courage and endurance of the world. When you read Article Ten, therefore, you will see that it is nothing but the inevitable, logical center of the whole system of the Covenant of the League of Nations, and I stand for it absolutely. If it should ever in any important respect be impaired, the glory of the armies and the navies of the United States is gone like a dream in the night, and there ensues upon it, the nightmare of dread which lay upon the nations before this war came; and there will come sometime, in the vengeful Providence of God, another struggle in which, not a few hundred thousand fine men from America will have to die, but as many millions as are necessary to accomplish the final freedom of the peoples of the world.

ORDERING OUR ARMIES ABROAD

Gentlemen would have you believe that our armies can be ordered abroad by some other power or by a combination of powers. America is not the only proud nation in the world. I can testify from my share in the counsels on the other side of the sea that the other nations are just as jealous of their sovereignty as we are of ours. They would no more have dreamed of giving us the right of ordering out their armies than we would have dreamed of giving them the right to order out our armies. The advice cannot be given without a unanimous vote of the Council of the League. Article Ten has no operative force in it unless we vote that it shall operate. The member of the Council representing the United States has to vote "aye" before the United States or any other country can be advised to go to war under that agreement, unless the United States is herself a party.

What does that mean? A party to what? A party to seizing somebody else's territory? A party to infringing some other country's political independence? I challenge any man to stand up before an American audience and say that that is the danger. Ah, but somebody else may seek to seize our territory or impair our political independence. Well, who? In looking about me I do not see anybody that would think it wise to try it on us. Who has an arm long enough, who has an audacity great enough to try to take a single inch of American territory or to seek to interfere for one moment with the political independence of the United States? But suppose we are parties; then is it the council of the League that is forcing war upon us? The war is ours anyhow. We are in circumstances where it is necessary for Congress, if it wants to steal somebody's territory or prevent somebody from stealing our territory to go to war. It is not the Council of the League that brings us into war at that time, in such circumstances. It is the unfortunate circumstances which have arisen in some matter of aggression. Then the war is ours anyhow. If we are a party we are in trouble already, and if we are not a party we can control the advice of the Council by our own vote.

There is no compulsion upon us to take that advice except the compulsion of our good conscience and judgment. So that it is perfectly evident that if, in the judgment of the people of the United States the Council adjudged wrong and that this is not a case of the use of force, there would be no necessity on the part of the Congress of the United States to vote the use of force. But let us suppose that it means something else; let us suppose there is some legal compulsion behind that advice. There could be no advice of the Council on any subject without a unanimous vote, and the unanimous vote includes our own, and if we accepted the advice we would be accepting our own advice, for I need not tell you the representatives of the Government of the United States would not vote without instructions from their government at home, and what we united in advising we could be certain that the American people would desire to do. I am not afraid of advice we give ourselves. There is in that Covenant not only not a surrender of the independent judgment of the Government of the United States but an expression of it because that independent judgment would have to join with the judgment of the rest. Whether we use it wisely or unwisely, we can use the vote of the United States to make impossible drawing the United States into any enterprise that she does not care to be drawn into.

We are free to exercise it in two stages. We are free to exercise it in the vote of our representative on the Council, who will, of course, act under instructions from the home government; and in the second place, we are to exercise it when the President, acting upon the action of the Council, makes his recommendations to Congress. Then the Congress is to exercise its judgment as to whether the instructions of the Executive to our member of the Council were well founded or not, and whether this is a case of distinct moral obligation. The men who were discussing these very important matters were all of the time aware that it would depend upon the approving or disapproving state of opinion of their countries how their representatives in the Council would vote in matters of this sort. It is inconceivable to me that unless the opinion of the United States, the moral and practical judgments of the people of the United States approved, the representatives of the United States on the Council should vote any such advice as would lead us into war.

Nothing could have been made more clear to the Conference than the right of our Congress under our Constitution to exercise its independent judgment in all matters of peace and war. No attempt was made to question that right. There is no sacrifice in the slightest degree of the independent choice of the Congress of the United States whether it will declare war or not. The United States will indeed undertake, under Article Ten, to "respect and preserve as against external aggression the territorial integrity and existing political independence of all members of the League," and that engagement constitutes a very grave and solemn moral obligation. But it is a moral, not a legal obligation, and leaves our Congress absolutely free to put its own interpretations upon it in all cases that call for action. In other words it is an attitude of comradeship and protection among the members of the League which in its very nature is moral and not legal. In every moral obligation there is an element of judgment. In a legal obligation there is no element of judgment. It is binding in conscience only, not in law; so that any way you turn Article Ten, it does not alter in the least degree the freedom and independence of the United States with regard to its action in respect of war. The United States cannot be drawn into anything it does not wish to be drawn into, but the United States ought not to be itself in the position of saying, "You need not expect of us that we assume the same moral obligations that you assume. You need not expect of us that we will respect and preserve the territorial integrity and political independence of other nations."

PROTECTING THE PHILIPPINES

We have a problem ahead of us that ought to interest us in this connection. We have promised the people of the Philippine Islands that we will set them free, and it has been one of our perplexities how we should make them safe after we set them free. Before this conference at Paris, the only thing that could be suggested was that we should get a common guaranty from all the nations of the world that the Philippines should be regarded as neutral, just as Belgium was once regarded as neutral, and that they should guarantee her inviolability, because it was certainly to be expected that she would not be powerful enough to take care of herself against those who might wish to commit aggression against her. Under this arrangement it will be safe from the outset. They will become members of the League of Nations, every great nation in the world will be pledged to respect and preserve against external aggression from any quarter the territorial integrity and political independence of the Philippines. It simplifies one of the most perplexing problems that has ever faced the American public, but it does not simplify our problems merely; it illustrates the triumph of the American spirit.

HOW THE LEAGUE WILL CONSTRUE ARTICLE TEN

Gentlemen say, "We do not want the United States drawn into every little European squabble. Of course we do not, and under the League of Nations it is entirely within our choice whether we will be or not. The normal processes of the action of the League are certainly to be this. When trouble arises in the Balkans, when somebody sets up a fire somewhere in Central Europe among those little nations, which are for the time being looking upon one another with a good deal of jealousy and suspicion, because the passions of the world have not cooled—whenever that happens, the Council of the League will confer as to the best methods of putting out the fire. If you want to put out a fire in Utah, you do not send to Oklahoma for the fire engines. If you want to put out a fire in the Balkans, if you want to stamp out the smouldering flames in some part of Central Europe, you do not send to the United States for troops. The Council of the League selects the powers which are most ready, most available, most suitable, and selects them only at their own consent, so that the United States would in no such circumstances conceivably be drawn in unless the flame spread to the world; and would they then be left out, even if they were not members of the League? You have seen the fire spread to the world once, and did you not go in? If you saw it spread again, if you saw human liberty again imperilled, would you wait to be a member of the League to go in? In a war which imperils the just arrangements of mankind, America, the greatest, richest, freest people in the world must take sides. We could not live without taking sides. If the fight is big enough to draw the United States in, I predict they will be drawn in anyhow, and if it is not big enough to bring them in inevitably, they can go in or stay out according to their own decision. If that is not an open and shut security, I do not know of any. Yet that is Article Ten![1]

[1]See Appendix E.

THE MONROE DOCTRINE

One of the other suggestions I carried to Paris was that the Committees of the two Houses did not find the Monroe Doctrine safeguarded in the Covenant of the League of Nations. I suggested that to the conference in Paris, and they at once inserted the provision which is now there that nothing in that Covenant shall be construed as affecting the validity of the Monroe Doctrine. I do not see what more you can say. Can you?

I want you to realize how extraordinary that provision is. That is the most extraordinary sentence in that Treaty, for this reason: Up to that time there was not a nation in the world that was willing to admit the validity of the Monroe Doctrine. The rest of the world always looked askance on the Monroe Doctrine. Great Britain did not like the Monroe Doctrine as we grew big. It was one thing to have our assistance and another thing for us not to need her assistance.

Every nation in the world had been jealous of the Monroe Doctrine, had studiously avoided doing or saying anything that would admit its validity, and here are all the great nations of the world signing a document which admits its validity. By a sudden turn in the whole judgment of the world the Monroe

Doctrine was accepted by all the great powers of the world. It not only is not impaired but it has the backing of the world. That constitutes nothing less than a moral revolution in the attitude of the rest of the world toward America.

What is the validity of the Monroe Doctrine? The Monroe Doctrine means that if any outside power, any power outside this Hemisphere, tries to impose its will upon any portion of the Western Hemisphere, the United States is at liberty to act independently and alone in repelling the aggression; that it does not have to wait for the action of the League of Nations; that it does not have to wait for anything but the action of its own Administration and its own Congress. The Monroe Doctrine says that if anybody tries to interfere with affairs in the Western Hemisphere it will be regarded as an unfriendly act to the United States—not to the rest of the world—and that means that the United States will look after it, and will not ask anybody's permission to look after it. The document says that nothing in this document is to be construed as interfering with that. Could anything be plainer than that? Nothing can henceforth embarrass the policy of the United States in applying the Monroe Doctrine according to her own judgment.

[91]

And at last, in the Covenant of the League of Nations, the Monroe Doctrine has become the doctrine of the world. Not only may no European power impair the territorial integrity or interfere with the political independence of any State in the Americas, but no power anywhere may impair the territorial integrity or invade the political independence of another power. The principle that Mr. Canning suggested to Mr. Monroe has now been vindicated by its adoption by the representatives of mankind.

DOMESTIC QUESTIONS

In the next place they are afraid that other nations will interfere in our domestic questions. There, again the Covenant of the League distinctly says that if any dispute arises which is found to relate to an exclusively domestic question, the council shall take no action with regard to it, and make no report concerning it, and the questions that these gentlemen most often mention, namely the questions of the tariff and of immigration and of naturalization are acknowledged by every authoritative student of international law without exception, to be, as of course, domestic questions. These gentlemen want us to make an obvious thing painfully obvious by making a list of domestic questions, and I object to making a list for this very reason, that if you make a list you may leave something out. I remind all students of the law of the old principle of the law that the mention of one thing is the exclusion of other things; that if you meant everything, you ought to have said everything; that if you said a few things you did not have the rest in mind.

I object to making a list of domestic questions, because a domestic question may come up which I did not think of. For example, they have been very much worried at the phrase that nothing in the document shall be taken as impairing in any way the validity of such regional understandings as the Monroe Doctrine. They say, "Why put in 'such regional understandings as'"? What other understandings are there? Have you got something up your sleeve? Is there going to be a Monroe Doctrine in China? Why, the phrase was written in perfect innocence. The men with whom I was associated said, "It is not wise to put a specific thing that belongs only to one nation in a document like this. We do not know of any other regional understandings like it; we never heard of any other; we never expect to hear of any other, but there might some day be some other, and so we will say, 'such regional understandings as the Monroe Doctrine,'" and their phase was intended to give right of way to the Monroe Doctrine in the Western Hemisphere. In every such case the United States would be just as secure in her independent handling of the question as she is now. There is no obscurity whatever in this Covenant with regard to the safeguarding of the United States, along with other sovereign countries, in the control of domestic questions. Throughout these conferences it was necessary at every turn to safeguard the sovereign independence of the several governments who were taking part in the conference, and they were just as keen to protect themselves against outside intervention in domestic matters as we were. Therefore the whole-heartedness of their concurrent opinion runs with this safeguarding of domestic questions.

SIX VOTES OF THE BRITISH EMPIRE

There is another matter. They say the British Empire has six votes and we have only one. The answer to that is that it is most carefully arranged that our one vote equals the six votes of the British Empire. The justification for the representation of more than one part of the British Empire was that the British Empire is made up of semi-independent pieces, as no other empire in the world is. You know how Canada, for example, passes her own tariff law, does what she pleases to inconvenience the trade of the mother country.

Somebody has said that this Covenant was an arrangement for the dominance of Great Britain, and he based that upon the fact that in the Assembly of the League there are six representatives of the various parts of the British Empire. There are really more than that, because each member of the Assembly has three representatives, but six[1] units of the British Empire are represented, whereas the United States is represented as only one unit.

Anybody who will take the pains to read the Covenant of the League of Nations will find out that the Assembly, and it is only in the Assembly that the British Empire has six votes, is not a voting body. I am perfectly content to have only one when the one counts six, and that is exactly the arrangement under the League. I do not want to be a repeater— if my one vote goes, I do not want to repeat it five times.

Let us examine the matter a little more particularly. Besides the vote of Great Britain herself, the other five votes are the votes of Canada, of South Africa, of Australia, of New Zealand and of India. We ourselves were champions of giving a vote to Panama and of

[1]With Ireland admitted to the League in September, 1923, the British Empire will have seven votes.   H.F.

giving a vote to Cuba. I ask you in debating the affairs of mankind, would it have been fair to give Panama a vote, as she will have, Cuba a vote, both of them very much under the influence of the United States, and not give a vote to the Dominion of Canada? Do you not think that that fine Dominion has been a very good neighbor? Do you not think she is a good deal more like the United States than she is like Great Britain? Is not Canada more likely to agree with the United States than with Great Britain? Do you not feel that probably you think alike?

Do you think it unjust that that little Republic down in South Africa, whose gallant resistance to be subjected to any outside authority at all, we admired for so many months and whose fortunes we followed with such interest, should have the right to stand up and talk before the world? They talked once with their arms, and if I may judge by my contact with them, they can talk with their minds! Great Britain obliged South Africa to submit to her sovereignty, but she immediately after felt that it was convenient and right to hand the whole self-government of that colony over to the very men whom she had beaten. The representatives of South Africa in Paris were two of the most distinguished generals of the Boer Army, two of the realest men I ever met, two men that could talk sober counsel and wise advice along with the best statesmen of Europe. They were men who spoke frank counsel. To exclude General Botha and General Smuts from the right to stand up in the Parliament of the World, and say something concerning the affairs of mankind, would be absurd.

Do you think that it was unjust that Australia should be allowed to stand up and take part in the debate—Australia from which we have learned some of the most useful progressive policies of modern time, a little nation only five million in a great continent, but counting for several times five in its activities and in its interest in liberal reform. Do you not know how Australia has led the free people of the world in many matters that have led to social and industrial reform? It is one of the most enlightened communities in the world and absolutely free to choose its own way of life, independent of the British authority, except in matters of foreign relationship. When I was in Paris the men I could not tell apart, except by their hats, were the Americans and the Australians. They both had the swing of the fellows who say, "The gang is all here, what,—do we care?"

Could we deny a vote to that other little self-governing nation, for it practically is such in everything but its foreign affairs—New Zealand—or to that great voiceless multitude, that throng hundreds of millions strong in India?

I want to testify that some of the wisest and most dignified figures in the Peace Conference at Paris came from India—men who seemed to carry in their minds an older wisdom than the rest of us had, whose traditions ran back into so many of the unhappy fortunes of mankind that they seemed very useful counsellors as to how some ray of hope and some prospect of happiness could be opened to its people. I am willing that India should stand up in the councils of the world and say something.

I am willing that speaking parts should be assigned to these self-governing, self-respecting, and energetic portions of the great body of humanity. Would you want to deprive these great communities of a voice in the debate? It is a proposition that has never been stated, because to state it, answers it.

But having given these six votes, what are the facts? You have been misled with regard to them. Disputes can arise only through the governments which have international representation. In other words, diplomatically speaking, there is only one British Empire. The parts of it are but pieces of the whole.

The dispute, therefore, would be between the United States as a diplomatic unit and the British Empire as a diplomatic unit. That is the only ground upon which the two nations could deal with one another, whether by way of dispute or agreement. They cannot out-vote us. These six votes are in the Assembly, not in the Council. There is only one thing that the Assembly votes on in which it can de-cide a matter without the concurrence of all the states represented on the Council, and that is the admission of new members to the League of Nations. With the single exception of admitting new members to the League there is no energy in the six votes which is not offset by the energy in the one vote of the United States and I am more satisfied to be one and count six than to be six and count only six. With regard to every other matter, for exam-ple, amendments to the Covenant, with re-gard to cases referred out of the Council to the Assembly, it is provided that if a majority of the Assembly and the representatives of all the States represented on the Council concur, the vote shall be valid and conclusive, which means that the affirmative vote of the United States is in every instance just as powerful as the six votes of the British Empire. There is no validity in a vote by the Council or the As-sembly, in which we do not concur. I took the pains to go through the Covenant almost sentence by sentence again, to find if there was any case other than the one I have mentioned, in which that was not true, and there is no other case in which that is not true. No active policy can be undertaken by the League without the assenting vote of the United States. I think that is a perfectly safe situation!

Of course, you will understand that wherever the United States is a party to a quarrel and that quarrel is carried to the Assembly, we cannot vote; similarly, if the British Empire is a party, her six representatives cannot vote. It is an even break any way you take it, and I would rather count six as one person than six as six persons. So far as I can see, it makes me a bigger man. The point to remember is that the energy of the League of Nations resides in the Council, not in the Assembly, and that in the Council there is a perfect equality of votes. The six votes of the British Empire are offset by our own, if we choose to offset them. I dare say we shall often agree with them, but if we do not, they cannot do anything to which we do not consent. This thing that has been talked about is a delusion. The United States is not easily frightened, and I dare say it is least easily frightened by things that are not true.

Let us be big enough to know the facts and

to welcome the facts, because the facts are based upon the principle that America has always fought for, namely, the equality of self-governing peoples, whether they were big or little—not counting men, but counting rights, not counting representation, but counting the purpose of that representation. When you hear an opinion quoted, you do not count the number of persons who hold it; you ask, "Who said that?" You weigh opinions, you do not count them, and the beauty of all democracies is that every voice can be heard, every voice can have its effect, every voice can contribute to the general judgment that is finally arrived at. That is the object of democracy. Let us accept what America has always fought for, and accept it with pride that America showed the way and made the proposal. I do not mean that America made the proposal in this particular instance; I mean that the principle was an American principle, proposed by America.

ARTICLE ELEVEN

I want you to notice another interesting point that is never dilated upon in connection with the League of Nations. I want to call your attention to Article Eleven, following Article Ten, of the Covenant of the League of Nations. That article is the favorite article in the

Treaty, so far as I am concerned. Under Article Eleven, any member of the League can at any time call attention to anything, anywhere, which is likely to disturb the peace of the world or the good understanding between nations upon which the peace of the world depends. This Covenant makes it the right of the United States and not the right of the United States merely, but the right of the weakest nation in the world to bring anything that the most powerful nation in the world is doing that is likely to disturb the peace of the world under the scrutiny of mankind. The smallest nation along with the largest—Panama—to take one of our near neighbors—can stand up and challenge the right of any nation in the world to do anything which threatened the peace of the world. It does not have to be a big nation to do it. Nothing is going to keep this world fit to live in like exposing in public every crooked thing that is going on. The peace of the world is everybody's business. If you think a policy good you will venture to talk about it. If you think it is bad, you will not consent to talk about it. You can not afford to discuss a thing when you are in the wrong, and the minute you feel that the whole judgment of the world is against you, you have a different temper in affairs altogether. The weak and oppressed and wronged peoples of the world have never before had a forum made for them in which they can summon their enemies into the presence of the judgment of mankind, and if there is one tribunal that the wrongdoer ought to dread more than another, it is that tribunal of the opinion of mankind.

You remember those immortal words in the opening part of the Declaration of Independence, "that out of respect to the opinion of mankind the causes which have led the people of the American colonies to declare their independence are here set forth"! America was the first country in the world which laid before all mankind the reason why it went to war. America was the first to set that example, the first to admit that right and justice and even the basis of revolution was a matter upon which mankind is entitled to form a judgment, and this Treaty is the exaltation and permanent establishment of the American principle of warfare and of right.

INTERNATIONAL LAW COMPLETELY CHANGED

What is the international law? International law up to this time has been the most singular code of manners. You could not mention to any other government anything that concerned it unless you could prove that your own interests were involved. International law is that no matter how deeply the United States is interested in something in some other part of the world, that she believes is going to set the world on fire or disturb the friendly relations between two great nations, she cannot speak of it unless she can show that her own interests are directly involved. It is a hostile and unfriendly act to call attention to it, and Article Eleven says, in so many words, that it shall be the friendly right of every nation to call attention to any such matters anywhere. In other words, at present, we have to mind our own business. Under the Covenant of the League of Nations we can mind other people's business and everything that affects the peace of the world, whether we are parties to it or not, can by our delegates be brought to the attention of mankind. We can force a nation on the other side of the globe to bring to that bar of mankind any wrong that is afoot in that part of the world which is likely to affect the good understanding between nations, and we can oblige them to show cause why it should not be remedied. There is not an oppressed people in the world which cannot henceforth get a hearing at that forum, and you know what a hearing will mean if the cause of those people is just. The one thing that those who are doing injustice have most to dread is publicity and discussion, because if you are challenged to give a reason why you are doing a wrong thing it has to be an exceedingly good reason, and if you give a bad reason you confess judgment and the opinion of mankind goes against you.

When anybody of kin to us in America is done wrong by any foreign government, it is likely to disturb the good understanding between nations upon which the peace of the world depends, and thus anyone of the causes represented in the hearts of the American people can be brought to the attention of the whole world. Every people in the world that have not got what they think they ought to have is thereby given a world forum in which to bring the thing to the bar of mankind. An incomparable thing—a thing that never was dreamed of before. A thing that was never conceived as possible before—that it should not be regarded as an unfriendly act on the part of the representatives of one nation to call attention to something being done within the confines of another empire which was disturbing the peace of the world and the good understanding between nations. One of the most effective means for winning a good cause is to bring it before that great jury. The only case that you ought to bring with diffidence before the great jury of men throughout the world is the case that you cannot establish. A bad cause will fare ill, but a good cause is bound to be triumphant in such a forum. You dare not lay a bad cause before mankind. You dare not kill the young men of the world for a dishonest purpose. It is not only we who are caught in the implications of the affairs of the world, everybody is caught in it now and it is right that anything that affects the world should be made everybody's business.

Discussion is destructive when wrong is intended; and all the nations of the world agree to put their case before the judgment of mankind. The nations of the world have declared that they are not afraid of the truth; that they are willing to have all their affairs that are likely to lead to international complications brought into the open. There never before has been provided a world forum in which the legitimate grievances of peoples entitled to consideration can be brought to the common judgment of mankind, and if I were the advocate of any suppressed or oppressed people, I surely could not ask any better forum than to stand up before the world and challenge the other party to make good its excuses for not acting in that case. That compulsion is the most tremendous moral compulsion that could be devised by organized mankind. Human beings can get together by discussion, and it is the business of civilization to get together by discussion and not by fighting. That is civilization. That has been the dream of thoughtful reformers for generation after generation; that the peace of the world transcends all the susceptibilities of nations and governments, and that they are obliged to consent to discuss and explain anything which does affect the understanding between nations. That in itself constitutes a revolution in international relationships. All forward-looking men may now see their way to the method in which they may help forward the real process of civilization.[1]

SECRET TREATIES

There can hereafter be no secret treaties. From this time forth all the world is going to know what all the agreements between nations are. It is going to know, not their general character merely, but their exact language and contents.

This Covenant cures one of the principal difficulties we encountered at Paris. At every turn in these discussions we came across some secret treaty, some understanding that had never been made public before, some understanding which embarrassed the whole settlement. It was very embarrassing when you

[1]Woodrow Wilson wrote Article Eleven.   H.F.

thought you were approaching an ideal solution of a particular question to find that some of your principal colleagues had given the whole thing away. I think it will not be improper for me to refer to one of them—the matter of the cession to Japan of the interest of Germany in Shantung, in China. I am not going to discuss the merits of that question, because it had no merits. The whole thing was bad. My present point is that there stood at the gate of that settlement a secret treaty between Japan and two of the great powers engaged in this war on our side. We could not ask them to disregard those promises. This war had been fought in part because of the refusal to observe the fidelity which is involved in a promise, because of the failure to regard the sacredness of treaties, and this Covenant of the League of Nations provides that no secret treaty shall have any validity. It provides in explicit terms that every treaty, every international understanding, shall be registered with the Secretary of the League; that it shall be published as soon as possible after it is there registered; and that no treaty that is not there registered will be regarded by any of the nations engaged in the Covenant. It is like our arrangements with regard to mortgages on real estate, that until they are registered nobody else need pay any attention to them; and so with the treaties—until they are registered in this office of the League, nobody, not even the parties themselves, can insist upon their execution. Just as you can go to the courthouse and see all the mortgages on all the real estate in your county, you can go to the general Secretariat of the League of Nations and find all the mortgages on all the nations. This Treaty, in short, is a great clearing house. It is very little short of a cancelling of the past and an insurance of the future.

You have cleared the deck thereby of the most dangerous thing and the most embarrassing thing that has hitherto existed in international politics. There were nations represented around that board—I mean the board at which the commission on the League of Nations sat, where fourteen nations were represented—there were nations represented around that board who had entered into many a secret treaty and understanding, and they made not the least objection to promising that hereafter no secret treaty should have any validity whatever. So that we not only have the right to discuss anything, but we make everything open for discussion. If this Covenant accomplished little more than the abolition of private arrangements between great powers, it would have gone far toward stabilizing the peace of the world and securing justice, which it has been so difficult to secure, so long as nations could come to secret understandings with one another. In other words, we have the pledge of all the nations of the world that they will sit down and talk everything over that is apt to make trouble amongst them, and that they will talk it over in public, so that the whole illuminating process of public knowledge and public discussion may penetrate every part of the conference. Everything is to be open. Everything is to be upon the table around which sit the representatives of all the world, the Asiatic, the African, the American, the European. That is the promise of the future; that is the security of the future.

SHANTUNG

That matter of the cession of certain German rights in Shantung Province in China, is connected with this Treaty but not with the League of Nations. I think that it is worth while to make that matter pretty clear, and I will ask you to be patient while I make a brief historical review in order to make it clear.

What happened under the old order of things? The story begins in 1898. What happened was that two German missionaries in China had been murdered. The central Government at Peking had done everything that was in its power to do to quiet the local disturbances, to allay the local prejudice against foreigners which led to the murders, but had been unable to do so, and the German Government held them responsible, nevertheless, for the murder of the missionaries. It was not the missionaries that the German Government was interested in; that was a pretext. It makes anybody who regards himself as a Christian blush to think what Christian nations have done in the name of protecting Christianity. That was what Germany did. She insisted that because of this thing happening, for which the Peking Government could not really with justice be held responsible, a very large and important part of one of the richest Provinces of China should be ceded to her for sovereign control, for a period of ninety-nine years, that she should have the right to penetrate the interior of that Province with a railway, and that she should have the right to exploit any ores that lay within thirty miles either side of that railway. There was no adequate excuse for what Germany exacted of China. I read again only the other day the phrases in which poor China was made to make the concessions. She was made to make them in words dictated by Germany, in view of her gratitude to Germany for certain services rendered—the deepest hypocrisy conceivable. She was obliged to do so by force.

That was the beginning. We are thinking so much about that concession to Germany, that we have forgotten that practically all of the great European powers had exacted similar concessions of China previously; they had already had their foothold of control in China; they had already had their control of railways; they already had their exclusive concessions over mines. Germany was doing an outrageous thing, I take the liberty of saying, as the others had done outrageous things, but it was not the first; at least, it had been done before. China lay rich and undeveloped and the rest of the world was covetous and it had made bargains with China, generally to China's disadvantage which enabled the world to go in and exploit her riches. Germany obliged China to give her what China had given others previously. Immediately thereafter China was obliged, because she had done this, to make fresh concessions to Great Britain of a similar sort, to make fresh concessions to France, to make concessions of a similar kind to Russia. It was then that she gave Russia Port Arthur and Talien-Wan.

Now remember what followed. The Government of the United States did not make any kind of protest against any of those concessions. No protest was made by the Government of the United States against the original cession of this Shantung territory to Germany. We had at that time one of the most public-spirited and humane men in the executive chair at Washington that have ever graced that chair—I mean William McKinley —and his Secretary of State was a man whom we have always delighted to praise, Mr. John Hay. But they made no protest against the cession to Germany, or to Russia or to Great Britain or to France. The only thing they insisted on was that none of those powers should close the doors of commerce to the goods of the United States in those territories which they were taking from China. You have heard of Mr. Hay's policy of the Open Door. That was his policy of the open door—not the open door to the right of China, but the open door to the goods of America. They took no interest, I mean so far as what they did was concerned, in the liberties and rights of China. They were interested only in the right of the merchants of the United States. They therefore, demanded and obtained promises that we could continue to sell merchandise in Shantung. Just so we could trade with those stolen territories we were willing to let them be stolen. All they asked was that Germany, after she got what did not belong to her, would please not close the door against the trade of the United States. I am not saying this by way of criticism. I want to hasten to add that I do not say this even to imply criticism on these gentlemen. That is all that under international manners they had a right to ask. I believe Mr. Hay, if he had seen any way to accomplish more than he did accomplish, would have attempted to do so.

Why did not Mr. Hay protest the acquisition of those rights in Shantung by Germany? Why did he not protest what England got, and what France got and what Russia got? Because under international law, as it then stood, that would have been a hostile act towards those governments. The law of the world was actually such that if you mentioned anybody else's wrong but your own, you spoke as an enemy. They could not lift a little finger to help China. They could only try to help the trade of the United States. Until this Treaty was written in Paris it was not even proposed that it should be the privilege of anybody to protest in any such case if his own rights were not directly affected.

Then came the war between Russia and Japan, and what happened? Japan did what she has done in this war. She attacked Port Arthur and captured it. You remember where that war was brought to a close—by delegates of the two powers sitting at Portsmouth, N. H., at the invitation of Mr. Roosevelt, who was then President. In a treaty signed on our own sacred territory, at Portsmouth in New Hampshire, Japan was allowed to take from Russia what had belonged to China, the concession of Port Arthur and of Talien-Wan, the territory in that neighborhood. The treaty was written here, it was written under the auspices, so to say, of our own public opinion, but the Government of the United States was not at liberty to protest and did not protest; it acquiesced in the very thing which is being done in this Treaty. What is being done in this Treaty is not that Shantung is being taken from China. China did not have it! It is being taken from Germany, just as Port Arthur was not taken from China, but taken from Russia and transferred to Japan.

Before we got into this war, but after the war had begun, because they deemed the assistance of Japan in the Pacific absolutely indispensable, Great Britain and France both agreed that if Japan would enter and cooperate in the war she could do the same thing with regard to Shantung that she had done with regard to Port Arthur; that if she would take what Germany had in China she could keep it. She took it! They were bound by a treaty of which we knew nothing, but which, notwithstanding our ignorance of it, bound them as much as any treaty binds. This war was fought to maintain the sacredness of treaties. Great Britain and France therefore, cannot consent to a change of the Treaty in respect of the cession of Shantung, and we have no precedent in our history which permits us even to protest against it until we become members of the League of Nations.

Well, you say, "Then, is it just all an ugly hopeless business?" It is not, if we adopt the League of Nations. The Government of the United States was not bound by these treaties. The Government of the United States was at liberty to get anything out of the bad business that it could get by persuasion and argument and it was upon the instance of the Government of the United States, that Japan promised to return to China what none of these other powers has yet promised to return—all rights of sovereignty that China had granted Germany over any portion of the Province of Shantung—the greatest concession in that matter that has ever been made by any power that has interested itself in the exploits of China, and to retain only what corporations out of many countries have long enjoyed in China, the right to run the railroad and extend its lines to certain points and to continue to work the mines that have already been opened. Scores of foreign corporations have that right in other parts of China. The only promise of that kind ever made, the only relinquishment of that sort ever achieved. That is her promise, and personally I have not the slightest doubt that she will fulfill that promise. But I said a minute ago, that Mr. Hay and Mr. McKinley were not at liberty to protest.

Turn to the League of Nations and see what will be the situation then. You will see that international law is revolutionized by putting morals into it. I want this point to sink in: The League of Nations changes the international law of the world with regard to matters of this sort. Japan solemnly undertakes with the rest of us, to protect the territorial integrity of China, along with the territorial integrity of other countries, and back of her promise lies the similar promise of every other nation, that nowhere will they countenance a disregard for the territorial integrity or the political independence of that great helpless people, lying there hitherto as an object of prey in the great Orient. It is the first time in the history of the world that anything has been done for China, and sitting around our council board in Paris I put this question: "May I expect that this will be the beginning of the retrocession to China of the exceptional rights which other governments have enjoyed there?" The responsible representatives of the other great governments said, "Yes, you may expect it." Expect it? What I want to call your attention to is just as soon as this Covenant is ratified every nation in the world will have the right to speak out for China; and I want to say very frankly, and I ought to add that the representatives of those great nations themselves admit, that Great Britain and France and the other powers which have insisted upon similar concessions in China will be put in a position where they will have to reconsider them. This is the only way to serve and redeem China, unless indeed, you want to start a war for that purpose!

You have heard a great deal about Article Ten of the Covenant of the League, but read Article Eleven in conjunction with Article Ten. Every member of the League, in Article Ten, agrees never to impair the territorial integrity of any other member of the League or to interfere with its existing political independence. Both of those things were done in all these concessions. There was a very serious impairment of the territorial integrity of China in every one of them, and a very serious interference with the political independence of that great but helpless kingdom. Article Ten stops that for good and all. Then in Article Eleven, it is provided that it shall be the friendly right of any member of the League at any time, to call attention to anything anywhere, that is likely to disturb the peace of the world or the good understanding between nations upon which the peace of the world depends; so that the ban would have been lifted from Mr. McKinley and Mr. Roosevelt in the matter of these things if we had the Covenant of the League; they could have gone in and said, "Here is your promise to preserve the territorial integrity and political independence of this great people. We have the friendly right to protest. We have the right to call your attention to the fact that this will breed wars and not peace, and that you have not the right to do this thing." Henceforth, for the first time, we shall have the opportunity to play effective friends to the great people of China. It is the most hopeful change in the law of the world that has been suggested or adopted. Are you willing to go into the great adventure of liberating hundreds of millions of human beings from the threat of foreign power? I, for one, am ready to do anything or to cooperate in anything in my power to be a friend, and a helpful friend, to that great, thoughtful, ancient, interesting, helpless people—in capacity, in imagination, in industry, in numbers one of the greatest peoples in the world and entitled to the wealth that lies underneath their feet and all about them in that land which they have not as yet known how to bring to its development.

If this Treaty is entered into by the United States, China will for the first time in her history have a forum in which to bring every wrong that is intended against her or that has been committed against her. And the alternative? If you insist upon cutting out the Shantung arrangement, that merely severs us from the Treaty. It does not give Shantung back to China. By being parties to that arrangement we can insist upon the promise of Japan—the promise which the other Governments have not matched—that she will return to China immediately all the sovereign rights within the Province of Shantung. We have got that for her now, and under the operations of Article Eleven and of Article Ten, it will be impossible for any nation to make any further inroads, either upon the territorial integrity or upon the political independence of China. If you are China's friend then put her in a position where even the concessions which have been made, need not be carried out. I am for helping China and not for turning away from the only way in which I can help her. Those are the facts about Shantung. Does the thing not look a little different?[1]

[1] The Department of State informs me it understands all Japanese troops were withdrawn from Shantung in December 1922. This corroborates Mr. Wilson's sentences that Japan would fulfill her withdrawal pledge.   H. F.

THE LEAGUE OF NATIONS

RESERVATIONS

The only thing that disturbs me, about the form which the opposition to the League is taking is this: Certain reservations as they are called, are proposed which in effect amount to this—that the United States is unwilling to assume the same obligations under the Covenant of the League as are assumed by the other members of the League; that the United States wants to disclaim any part in the responsibility which the other members of the League are assuming.

I want you to have a very clear idea of what is meant by reservations. Reservations are to all intents and purposes equivalent to amendments. What does a reservation mean? It means a stipulation that this particular government insists upon interpreting its duty under that Covenant in a special way, insists upon interpreting it in a way in which other governments, it may be, do not interpret it.

If all that you desire is to say what you understand this to mean, no harm can be done by saying it; but if you want to change the Treaty, if you want to alter the phraseology so that the meaning is altered, if you want to put in reservations which give the United States a position of special privilege or a special exemption from responsibility among the members of the League, then it will be necessary to take the Treaty back to the conference table, and the world is not in a temper to discuss this Treaty over again.

This thing when we ratify it, is a contract. You cannot alter so much as the words of a contract without the consent of the other parties. Any reservation will have to be carried to all the other signatories, Germany included, and we shall have to get the consent of Germany, among the rest, to read this Covenant in some special way in which we prefer to read it in the interest of the safety of America.

In order to put this matter in such a shape as will lend itself to concrete illustration, let me show you what I understand is a proposed form of reservation:

"The United States assumes no obligation under the provisions of Article Ten to preserve the territorial integrity or political independence of any other country or to interfere in controversies between other nations, whether members of the League or not, or to employ the military and naval forces of the United States under any article of the Treaty for any purpose, unless in any particular case the Congress, which under the Constitution, has the sole power to declare war or authorize the employment of the military and naval forces of the United States, shall by act or joint resolution so declare."

In other words, what this proposes is this: That we should make no general promise, but leave the nations associated with us to guess in each instance what we were going to consider ourselves bound to do. We will not assume any obligations. We will not promise anything, but from time to time we may cooperate. Does the United States want to say to the nations with whom it stood in this great struggle, "We have seen you through on the battlefield, but now we are done. We are not going to stand by you!"

Every war of any consequence that you can cite, originated in an attempt to seize the territory or interfere with the political independence of some other nation. We went into this war with the sacred promise that we regarded all nations as having the same rights, whether they were weak or strong, and unless we engage to sustain the weak we have guaranteed that the strong will prevail; we have guaranteed that the imperialistic enterprise will revive; we have guaranteed that there is no barrier to the ambition of nations that have the power to dominate; we have abdicated the whole position of right and substituted the principle of might. That is the heart of the Covenant, and what are these gentlemen afraid of? Nothing can be done under that article of the Treaty without the consent of the United States. In every case where the League takes action the unanimous vote of the council of the League is necessary; the United States is a permanent member of the council of the League, and its affirmative vote is in every case necessary for every affirmative, or for that matter every negative action; so that neither the United States nor any other country can be advised to go to war for the redemption of that promise without the concurrent affirmative vote of the United States. If we cannot be obliged to do anything that we do not ourselves vote to do, why qualify our acceptance of a perfectly safe agreement?

Yet I hear gentlemen say that this is an invasion of our sovereignty. If it is anything it is an exaggeration of our sovereignty, because it puts our sovereignty in a way to put a veto on that advice being given to anybody. If you want to keep your own boys at home after this terrible experience, you will see that other boys elsewhere are kept at home. Our present sovereignty merely extends to making choice whether we will go to war or not, but this extends our sovereignty to saying whether other nations shall go to war or not. If that does not constitute a very considerable insurance against war, I would like somebody to write a provision which would! Because America is not going to refuse, when the other catastrophe comes, again to attempt to save the world, and having given this proof once, I pray God that we may not be given occasion to prove it again. We went into this war promising every loving heart in this country who had parted with the beloved youngster that we were going to fight a war which would make that sacrifice unnecessary again and we must redeem that promise or be of all men the most unfaithful.

There is no necessity for the last part of this reservation. Every public man, every statesman, in the world knows, and I say that advisedly, that in order that the United States should go to war it is necessary for the Congress to act. They do not have to be told that, but that is not what this resolution says. This resolution says that the United States assumes no obligation under the provisions of Article Ten to preserve the territorial integrity or the political independence of any other country—washes its hands of the whole business; says, "We do not want even to create the presumption that we will do the right thing. We do not want to be committed even to a great principle, but we want to say that every time a case arises the Congress will independently take it up as if there were no covenant and determine whether there is any moral obligation; and after determining that, determining whether it will act upon that moral obligation or not, it will act." In other words, that is an absolute withdrawal from the obligations of Article Ten. It means the rejection of the Treaty, nothing less. It means that the United States would take from under the structure its very foundations and support.

INTERPRETATIONS

It has been suggested in public debate and in private conference, that interpretations of the sense in which the United States accepts the engagements of the Covenant should be embodied in the instrument of ratification. There can be no reasonable objection to such interpretations accompanying the act of ratification, provided they do not form a part of the formal ratification itself. Speaking now of those which some men of high conscience and of high public purpose are seriously pressing in order that there may be no misunderstanding. It is perfectly feasible, if we put interpretations upon that Treaty which its language clearly warrants, to notify the other governments of the world that we do understand the Treaty in that sense. It is perfectly feasible to do that, and perfectly honorable to do that, because, mark you, nothing can be done under this Treaty through the instrumentality of the council of the League of Nations except by a unanimous vote. The vote of the United States will always be necessary, and it is perfectly legitimate for the United States to notify the other governments beforehand that its vote in the council of the League of Nations will be based upon such and such an understanding of the provisions of the Treaty. You can avoid a misunderstanding without qualifying the terms of the document, because as I have said and shall say again and again, America is at liberty as one of the voting members of the partnership to state how she understands the articles of partnership.

THE BROAD SCOPE OF THE LEAGUE

I want to point out to you what apparently has escaped the attention of some of the critics of the League of Nations that the heart of the League of Nations Covenant does not lie in any of the portions which have been discussed in public debate. You would think it just had three or four articles in it to hear some men talk about it. Well, there are twenty-six articles altogether, and all of them are about something else.

I want you to realize just what the Covenant of the League of Nations means, because in so many parts of the country men are drawing attention to little details in a way that destroys the whole perspective of the great plan, in a way that concentrates attention upon certain particulars.

I am going to take the liberty of reading you a list of the things which the nations adhering to the Covenant of the League of Nations undertake. I want to say by way of preface that it seems to me, and I am sure it will seem to you, not only an extraordinarily impressive list, but a list which was never proposed for the counsels of the world before.

It provides for the destruction of autocratic power as an instrument of international control, admitting only self-governing nations to the League of Nations. Had you ever been told that before? No nation is admitted to the League of Nations whose people do not control its government. That is the reason that we are making Germany wait. She says that henceforth her people are going to control her government, but we have got to wait and see. If they do control it she is as welcome to the League as anybody else, because we are not holding nations off. We are holding selfish groups of men off. We are not saying to peoples, "We do not want to be your comrades and serve you along with the rest of our fellow beings," but we are saying, "It depends upon your attitude; if you take charge of your own affairs, then come into the game and welcome." The League of Nations sends autocratic governments to coventry. That is the first point.

It provides for the substitution of publicity, discussion and arbitration for war. That is the supreme thing that it does.

Instead of using force after this period of discussion something very much more effective than force is proposed, namely, an absolute boycott of the nation that does not keep its covenant, and when I say an absolute boycott, I mean an absolute boycott.

It provides for placing the peace of the world under constant international oversight, in recognition of the principle that the peace of the world is the legitimate and immediate interest of every nation.

It provides for disarmament on the part of the great fighting nations of the world.

It provides in detail for the rehabilitation of oppressed peoples, and that will remove most of the causes of war.

It provides that there shall be no more annexations of territory anywhere, but that those territories whose people are not ready to govern themselves shall be intrusted to the trusteeship of the nations that can take care of them, the trustee nation to be responsible in annual report to the League of Nations; that is to say, to mankind in general, subject to removal and restricted in respect to anything that might be done to that population which would be to the detriment of the population itself. So that you cannot go into darkest Africa and make slaves of those poor people, as some governments at times have done.

It abolishes enforced labor. It takes the same care of the women and children of those unschooled races that we try to take of the women and children of ours.

It provides that every secret treaty shall be invalid. It sweeps the table of all private understandings and enforces the principle that there shall be no private understandings of any kind that anybody is bound to respect.

It provides for the protection of dependent peoples.

It provides that high standards of labor, such as are observed in the United States, shall be extended to the working man everywhere in the world.

It organizes a new method of cooperation among all the great Red Cross societies of the world. That simple red cross has come to mean to the world more than it ever meant before. Everywhere in the remotest recesses of the world—there are people who wear that symbol, and every time I look at it, I feel like taking off my hat, as if I had seen a symbol of the world's heart. This Treaty is nothing less than an organization of liberty and mercy for the world. It provides that all the great humane instrumentalities, like the conventions against the opium trade, like the regulation of the liquor traffic with debased and ignorant people, like the prohibition of the selling of arms and ammunition to people who can use them only to their own detriment, shall be under the common direction and control of the League of Nations.

That is the League of Nations. Nothing can be discussed there that concerns our domestic affairs. Nothing can be discussed there that concerns the domestic affairs of any other people unless something is occurring in some nation which is likely to disturb the peace of the world, and any time that any question arises which is likely to disturb the peace of the world, then the Covenant makes it the right of any member, strong or weak, big or little of that universal concert of the nations to bring that matter up for clarification and discussion. We shall not be drawn into wars; we shall be drawn into consultation, and we will be the most trusted adviser in the whole group. Consultation, discussion, is written all over the whole face of the Covenant of the League of Nations, for the heart of it is that the nations promise not to go to war until they have consulted, until they have discussed, until all the facts in the controversy have been laid before the court which represents the common opinion of mankind. Can you imagine anything more calculated to put war off, not only to put it off, but to make it violently improbable?

That being the case, it becomes sheer nonsense to talk about a supergovernment being set up over the United States; it becomes sheer nonsense to say any authority is constituted which can order our armies to other parts of the world, which can interfere with our domestic questions, which can direct our international policy even in any matter in which we do not consent to be directed. We would be under our own direction just as much under the Covenant of the League of Nations as we are now.

Of course, I do not mean to say that we do not, so to say, pool our moral issues. We do that. In acquiescing in the Covenant of the League we do adopt, as we should adopt, certain fundamental moral principles of right and justice, which I dare say, we do not need to promise to live up to, but which we are certainly proud to promise to live up to. We are not turning any corner. We always have lived up to them, and we do not intend to change our course of action or our standards of action. And it is American standards of action that are set up in the Covenant of the League of Nations.

THE HISTORY OF THE LEAGUE

There seems to have arisen an idea in some quarters that the League of Nations is an idea recently conceived, conceived by a small number of persons, somehow originated by the American representatives at the council table in Paris. You have been led to believe that the Covenant of the League of Nations is in some sense a private invention. It is not always said of whom, and I need not mention who is suspected! It is supposed that out of some sort of personal ambition or party intention, an authorship, an origination, is sought. Nothing could be further from the truth. I would not feel the confidence that I feel in the League of Nations if I felt that it was so recent and novel a growth and birth as that. Just as there was in America a league to enforce peace, which even formulated a constitution for the league of peace before the conference met, before the conference was thought of, before the war began, so there were in Great Britain, and in France, and in Italy, and, I believe, even in Germany, similar associations of equally influential men, whose ideal was that some time there might come an occasion when men would be sane enough and right enough to get together to do a thing of this great sort. I wish that I could claim the great distinction of having invented this great idea, but it is a great idea which has been growing in the minds of all generous men for several generations. Several generations? Why, it has been the dream of the friends of humanity through all the ages, and now for the first time a great body of practical statesmen, immersed in all the business of individual nations, gets together and realizes the dream of honest men. I wish that I could claim some originative part in so great an enterprise, but I cannot. I had the great privilege of being the spokesman of this splendid Nation at this critical period in her history, but I was her spokesman, not my own, and when I advocated the things that are in this League of Nations I had the full and proud consciousness that I was only expressing the best thought of my fellow countrymen.

The only things that I have any special personal connection with in the League of Nations Covenant are things that I was careful to have put in there because of the very considerations which are now urged. I did have a part in some of the phraseology. For example, there is one part of the Covenant, the principal part of it, where it speaks of arbitration and discussion, where it provides that any member state, failing to keep these particular covenants shall be regarded as thereby ipso facto to have committed an act of war against the other members. The way it originally read was "Shall thereby ipso facto be deemed at war with the other members," and I said, "No, I cannot agree to that. That provision would put the United States at war without the consent of the Congress of the United States, and I have no right in this part of the Covenant or any other part, to assent to a provision which would deprive the Congress of the United States of its free choice whether it makes war or not." There and at every other point in the Covenant where it was necessary to do so, I insisted upon language which would leave the Congress of the United States free, and yet gentlemen say that the Congress of the United States is deprived of its liberty. I fought that battle and won it. It is not necessary for them to fight it over again. I was the spokesman in this matter, so far as I was influential at all, of all sorts and kinds of Americans, of all parties and factions in America.

EMINENT REPUBLICANS AND THE LEAGUE

Some of the greatest spirits, some of the most instructed minds of both parties have been devoted to this great idea for more than a generation. When I went to Paris I was conscious that I was carrying there no plan which was novel either to America or to Europe, but a plan which all statesmen who realized the real interests of their people had long ago hoped might be carried out in some day when the world would realize what the peace of the world meant and what were its necessary foundations. I was merely the spokesman of thoughtful and of hopeful spirits in America.

What I want everybody in every American audience to understand is this—the first effective impulse toward this sort of thing came from America, and I want to call your attention to the fact that it came from some of the very men who are now opposing its consummation. They dreamed the dream that has now been realized. They saw the vision twenty, twenty-five, thirty years ago which all mankind are now permitted to see. I, along with thousands of my fellow countrymen, got the idea twenty years ago, chiefly from Republican public men. Take men like ex-Senator Burton, of Ohio. He has been preaching a League of Nations for twenty years.

Some very interesting things happened while we were on the other side of the water. One of the most distinguished lawyers in the United States, Mr. Wickersham of New York, who was Attorney General in Mr. Taft's cabinet, came over to Europe—I am told, I did not see him while he was over there—to oppose the things he understood the American peace commission was trying to accomplish, and what happened to Mr. Wickersham? He was absolutely converted, above all things else, to the necessity for a League of Nations not only, but for this League of Nations. He came back to the United States and has ever since, in season and out of season, been preaching in public advocacy of the adoption of this Covenant. I need not tell you of the conspicuously fine work which his chief, Mr. Taft, has been doing in the same cause.[1]

It is of particular importance to remember, at this moment when some men have dared to introduce party passion into this discussion that some of the leading spirits, perhaps I may say the leading spirits in the conception of this great idea were the leading figures of the great Republican party. I say that not because it seems to me to make the least difference among Americans in a great matter like this, which party such things come from, but because I want to emphasize in every discussion of this matter, the absolutely non-partisan character of the Covenant and of the Treaty. I am particularly interested to have

See Appendix D.

you realize there is no politics in this business, except the profoundly important politics of civilization. I would be ashamed of myself, as I am frankly ashamed of any fellow country-man of mine who does it, if I discussed this great question with any portion of my thought devoted to the contest of parties and the elections of next year. There is one thing that is so much greater than being a Republican or a Democrat that those names ought never to be mentioned in connection with, and that is being an American. If anybody discusses this question on the basis of party advantage, I repudiate him as a fellow American; and in order to validate what I have said, I want to make one or two quotations from representatives of a party to which I do not belong.

The first I shall make from a man who has for a long time been a member of the United States Senate. In May 1916, just about two years after the Great War began, this Senator, at a banquet at which I was myself present, uttered the following sentences:

"I know, and no one I think can know better than one who has served long in the Senate, which is charged with an important share of the ratification and confirmation of all treaties, no one can, I think, feel more deeply than I do the difficulties which confront us in the work which this League—that is the great association extending throughout the country known as the League to Enforce Peace—undertakes, but the difficulties cannot be overcome unless we try to overcome them. I believe much can be done. Probably it will be impossible to stop all wars, but it certainly will be possible to stop some wars, and thus diminish their number. The way in which this problem is to be worked out must be left to this League and to those who are giving this great subject the study which it deserves. I know the obstacles. I know how quickly we shall be met with the statement that this is a dangerous question which you are putting into your agreement, that no nation can submit to the judgment of other nations, and we must be careful at the beginning not to attempt too much. I know the difficulties which arise when we speak of anything which seems to involve an alliance, but I do not believe that when Washington warned us against entangling alliances, he meant for one moment that we should not join with the other civilized nations of the world if a method could be found to diminish war and encourage peace.

"It was a year ago," he continues, "in delivering the chancellor's address at Union College, I made an argument on this theory, that if we were to promote international peace at the close of the present terrible war, if we were to restore international law as it must be restored, we must find some way in which the united forces of the nations could be put behind the cause of peace and law. I said then that my hearers might think that I was picturing a Utopia, but it is in the search for Utopias that great discoveries have been made. Not failure, but low aim is the crime. This League certainly has the highest of all aims for the benefit of humanity, and because the pathway is sown with difficulties is no reason that we should turn from it."

The quotation is from Hon. Henry Cabot Lodge.

I read another quotation from one of the most energetic, practical and distinguished leaders of the Republican party:

"The one effective move for obtaining peace is by an agreement among all the great powers in which each should pledge itself not only to abide by the decisions of a common tribunal but to back its decisions by force. The great civilized nations should combine by solemn agreement in a great world league for the peace of righteousness; a court should be established. A changed and amplified Hague Court would meet the requirements, composed of representatives from each nation, whose representatives are sworn to act as judges in each case and not in a representative capacity."

Now that is Article Ten. He goes on and says this:

"The nations should agree on certain rights that should not be questioned, such as territorial integrity, their right to deal with their domestic affairs, and with such matters as whom they should admit to citizenship. All such guarantee each of their number in possession of these rights."

A very worthy utterance from Theodore Roosevelt! I am glad to align myself with such utterances as those. I subscribe to every word of them: and here in concrete form is the fulfillment of the plan which they advocate.

It is the greatest process of international conference and of international discussion ever conceived, and that is what we are trying to substitute for war. That is what we must substitute for war. In other words, the only way we can prevent the unspeakable thing from happening again is that the nations of the world should unite and put an irresistible force behind peace and order. There is only one conceivable way to do that, and that is by means of a League of Nations. The very description is a definition of a League of Nations, and the only thing we can debate now is whether the nations of the world having

met in a universal congress and formulated a
Covenant as the basis for a League of Nations, we are going to accept that or insist
upon another. If we want a League of Nations, we must take this League of Nations
because there is no conceivable way in which
any other League of Nations is obtainable. I do
not find any man anywhere rash or bold
enough to say that he does not desire a League
of Nations. I only find men here and there
saying that they do not desire this League of
Nations, and I want to ask you to reflect upon
what that means; and in order to do that I
want to draw a picture for you, if you will be
patient with me, of what occurred in Paris.

In Paris were gathered the representatives
of nearly thirty nations from all over the civilized globe, and even from some parts of the
globe which in our ignorance of them we have
not been in the habit of regarding as civilized,
and out of that great body were chosen the
representatives of fourteen nations, representing all parts of the great stretches of the peoples of the world which the conference as a
whole, represented. The representatives of
those fourteen nations constituted a commission on the League of Nations.

The first resolution passed by the Conference of Peace in Paris was a resolution in favor

of a League of Nations, setting up a commission to formulate a League of Nations. It was the thought foremost in the mind of every statesman there. He knew that his errand was in vain in Paris if he went away without achieving the formation of a League of Nations, and that he dared not go back and face his people unless he could report that the efforts in that direction had been successful. That commission sat day after day, evening after evening. I had the good fortune to be a member of the commission, and I want to testify to the extraordinary good temper in which the discussions were conducted. I want to testify that there was a universal endeavor to subordinate as much as possible international rivalries and conflicting international interests and come out upon a common ground of agreement in the interest of the world. I want to testify that there were many compromises, but no compromises that sacrificed the principle, and that although the instrument as a whole represented certain mutual concessions, it is a constructive instrument and not a negative instrument. I shall never lose, as long as I live, the impression of generous, high-minded, statesmanlike cooperation which was manifested in that interesting body. It included representatives of all the most powerful nations, as well as representatives of some of those that were less powerful.

I could not help thinking as I sat there that the representatives of Italy spoke as it were in the tones of the long tradition of Rome; that we heard the great Latin people who had fought, fought, fought through generation after generation of strife down to this critical moment, speaking now in the counsels of peace; and there sat the prime minister of Greece—the ancient Greek people—lending his singular intelligence, his singularly high-minded and comprehensive counsel, to the general result. There were the representatives also of France, our ancient comrade in the strife for liberty; and there were the representatives of Great Britain, supposed to be the most ambitious, the most desirous of ruling the world of any of the nations of the world, cooperating with a peculiar interest in the result, with a constant and manifestly sincere profession that they wanted to subordinate the interests of the British Empire, which extended all over the world, to the common interests of mankind and of peace.

The representatives of Great Britain, I may stop to speak of for a moment. There were two of them. One of them was Lord Robert Cecil, who belongs to an ancient family in Great Britain, some of the members of which

—particularly Lord Salisbury of a past generation—had always been reputed as most particularly keen to seek and maintain the advantage of the British Empire; and yet I never heard a man speak whose heart was evidently more in the task of the humane redemption of the world than Lord Robert Cecil; and alongside of him sat General Smuts, the South African Boer, the man who had fought Great Britain so successfully, that after the war was over and the Boers nominally defeated, Great Britain saw that the wisest thing she could do was to hand the government of the country over to the Boers themselves. General Botha and General Smuts were both members of the peace conference; both had been successful generals in fighting the British arms. Nobody in the conference was more outspoken in criticizing some aspects of British policy than General Botha and General Smuts, and General Smuts was of the same mind with Sir Robert Cecil. They were both serving the common interests of free peoples everywhere.

You seem to see a sort of epitome of the history of the world in that conference. There were nations that had long been subordinated and suffering. There were nations that had long been indomitably free, but, nevertheless, not so free that they could really accomplish the objects that they had always held dear. I want you to realize that this conference was made up of many kinds and of many nations and of many traditions, keen to the same conclusion, with a unanimity, an enthusiasm, a spirit which speaks volumes for the future hopes of mankind. Is it not a great vision, this of the thoughtful world combined for peace, this of all the great peoples of the world associated to see that justice is done, that the strong who intend wrong are restrained and that the weak who cannot defend themselves are made secure?

It is the parliament of nations at last, where everyone is under covenant himself to do right, to respect and preserve the territorial integrity and existing political independence of the others, and where everyone engages never to go to war without first trying to settle the matter by the slow-cooling, disinterested processes of discussion. It is what we have been striving for for generation after generation, and now some men hesitate to accept it when the golden thing is placed in their hand.

What are we debating in the United States? Whether we will take part in guiding and steadying the world or not! And some men hesitate! It is the only country in the world whose leadership and guidance will be accepted! If we do not give it we may look forward to something like a generation of doubt and disorder which it will be impossible to pass through without the wreckage of a very considerable part of our slowly constructed civilization.

America and her determinations now constitute the balance of moral force in the world, and if we do not use that moral force we will be of all peoples the most derelict. We are in the presence of this great choice, whether we will stand by the mass of our own people and the mass of mankind.

AMERICA AND WORLD
PROBLEMS

~~~~~~

WE have come to one of the turning points in the history of the world, and what I as an American, covet for this great country is that, as on other great occasions when mankind's fortunes hung in a nice poise and balance, America may have the distinction to lead the way.

America and the world have come to the point where they must make one of the most critical choices ever made by great bodies of men or by nations. They have now to determine whether they will accept the one chance that has ever been offered to insure the peace of the world.

We are facing a decision now in which we cannot afford to make a mistake. We must not let ourselves be deceived as to the gravity of that decision or as to the implications of that decision. It will mean a great deal now, but it will mean infinitely more in the future. We are making decisions now which will mean more to the children than they mean to us, and as we care for the future generations, we will be careful to make the right decisions as to the policy of the United States as one of the factors in the peace of the world. America has to do at this moment nothing less than to prove to the world whether she has meant what she has said in the past. If we as a nation indeed mean what we have always said, that we are the champions of human right, now is the time when we shall be brought to the test, the acid test, as to whether we mean what we said or not.

Party politics has no place in the subject we are now obliged to discuss and to decide. Politics in the wider sense has a great deal to do with it. The politics of the world, the policy of mankind, the concert of the methods by which the world is to be bettered, that concert of will and of action which will make every nation a nobler instrument of Divine Providence—that is world politics.

I have sometimes heard gentlemen discussing the questions that are now before us with a distinction drawn between nationalism and internationalism. It is very difficult for me to follow their distinction. The greatest nationalist is the man who wants his nation to be the greatest nation, and the greatest nation is the nation that penetrates to the heart of its duty and mission among the nations of the world. With every flash of insight into the great politics of mankind, the nation that has that vision is elevated to a place of influence and power which it cannot get by arms, which it cannot get by commercial rivalry, which it can get by no other way than by that spiritual leadership which comes from a profound understanding of the problems of humanity.

If I am a true American I will study the true interests of America. If I am a true American I will have the world vision that America has always had, drawing her blood, drawing her genius, as she has drawn her people, out of all the great constructive peoples of the world. A true American conceives America in the atmosphere and whole setting of her fortune and her destiny.

You know when this nation was born and we were just a little group—3,000,000 people on the Atlantic coast—how the nations on the other side of the water and the statesmen of that day watched us with a certain condescension, looked upon us as a sort of group of hopeful children pleased for the time being with the conception of absolute freedom and political liberty, far in advance of the other peoples of the world because less experienced than they, less aware of the difficulties of the great task that they had accomplished. As the years have gone by they have watched the growth of this nation with astonishment and for a long time with dismay. They watched it with dismay until a very interesting and significant thing happened.

They have seen the United States do what no other nation ever did. When we fought the war with Spain there was many a cynical smile on the other side of the water when we said that we were going to win freedom for Cuba and then present it to her. When we fought Cuba's battle for her, then they said, "Ah, it is the beginning of what we predicted. She will seize Cuba, and after Cuba, what she pleases to the south of her. It is the beginning of the history we have gone through ourselves." They ought to have known; they set us the example! When we actually fulfilled to the letter, our promise that we would set helpless Cuba up as an independent government and guarantee her independence—when we carried out that great policy we astounded and converted the world. When we kept that promise and proved our absolute disinterestedness, and notwithstanding the fact that we had beaten Spain until she had to accept anything that we dictated, paid her $20,000,000 for something that we could have taken, namely, the Philippine Islands, all the world stood at amaze. Then began—let me repeat the word again—then began the confidence of the world in America.

I want you to recall the circumstance of

this great war lest we forget. We must not forget to redeem absolutely and without qualification the promises of America in this great enterprise. The principle that America went into this war for was the principle of the equality of sovereign nations. Our contention has always been, in international affairs, that we should deal with them upon the principle of the absolute equality of independent sovereignty. It has been a matter of principle with the United States to maintain that in respect of rights there was not and should be no difference between a weak State and a strong State.

I am just as much opposed to class legislation in international matters as in domestic matters. I do not, I tell you plainly, believe that any one nation should be allowed to dominate, even this beloved Nation of our own, and it does not desire to dominate. No sort of privilege will ever be permitted in this country. It is a partnership or it is a mockery. It is a democracy, where the majority are the masters, or all the hopes and purposes of the men who founded this government have been defeated and forgotten. And I am of the same principle in international affairs. One of the things that gave the world a new and bounding hope was that the great United States had said that it was fighting for the little nation as well as the great nation; that it regarded the rights of the little nation as equal to its own rights; that it would make no distinction between free men anywhere; that it was not fighting for a special advantage for the United States but for an equal advantage for all free men everywhere.

BREMEN TO BAGDAD

Turn your thoughts back to what it was that Germany proposed. The formula of Pan-Germanism was Bremen to Bagdad. What is the line from Bremen to Bagdad? It leads through partitioned Poland, through prostrated Roumania, through subjugated Slavia down through disordered Turkey, and on into distressed Persia, and every foot of the line is a line of political weakness. Germany was looking for the line of least resistance to establish her power, and unless the world makes that a line of absolute resistance this war will have to be fought over again. You must settle the difficulties which gave occasion to the war or you must expect war again. You know what happened all through that territory. Almost everywhere there were German princes planted on thrones where they did not belong, where they were alien, where they were of a different tradition and a different people, mere agents of a political plan, the seething center of which was that unhappy city of Constantinople, where, I dare say, there was more intrigue to the square inch than there has ever been anywhere else in the world, and where not the most honest minds always but generally the most adroit minds were sent to play upon the cupidity of the Turkish authorities and upon the helplessness of the Balkan States, in order to make a field for European aggression. I am not now saying that Germany was the only intriguer. I am not now saying that hers was the only plan of advantage, but I am saying that there was the field where lay the danger of the world in regard to peace.

Germany did direct her first force against France and against Belgium, but you know that it was not her purpose to remain in France, though it was part of her purpose to remain in Belgium. She was using her armies against these people so that they could not prevent what she intended elsewhere, and what she intended elsewhere was to make an open line of dominion between her and the Far East. The formula that she adopted was Bremen to Bagdad, the North Sea to Persia —to crush not only little Serbia, whom she first started to crush, but all the Balkan States, get Turkey in her grasp, take all the Turkish and Arabian lands beyond, penetrate the wealthy realms of Persia, open the gates of India, and, by dominating the central trade routes of the world, dominate the world itself. That was her plan. The Germans were travelling that road. The merchants and manufacturers and bankers of Germany were making conquest of the world. All they had to do was to wait a little longer, and long German fingers would have been stretched all through that country which never could have been withdrawn. German intrigue was penetrating all those countries and controlling them. Their general staff interrupted the game. The war spoiled the game.

The German people is a great educated people. All the thoughtful men in Germany, so far as I have been able to learn, who were following peaceful pursuits, deemed it folly to go into that war. They said so then and they have said so since. The business men of Germany did not want the war that we have passed through. The bankers and the manufacturers and the merchants knew that it was unspeakable folly. Why? Because Germany, by her industrial genius, was beginning to dominate the world economically, and all she had to do was to wait for about two more generations when her credit, her merchandise, her enterprise, would have covered all the parts of the world that the great fighting nations of the world did not control. But they were not consulted. The masters of Germany were the general military staff; it was these men who nearly brought a complete cataclysm upon civilization itself.

And now look what has happened: Poland, Bohemia, the released parts of Roumania, Jugo-Slavia—these could, none of them, have won their own independence any more than Cuba could have won hers, and they were under an authority just as reckless in the exercise of its force, just as regardless of the people and of humanity as the Spanish Government ever was in Cuba and the Philippines; and by the force of the world these people have been liberated. All down through the center of Europe and into the heart of Asia has gone this process of liberation, taking alien yokes off the necks of such peoples and vindicating the American principle that you cannot impose upon anybody a sovereignty that is not of its own choice.

Poland, Czecho-Slovakia, Roumania, Jugo-Slavia—all those nations which never had a vision of independent liberty until now—have their liberty and independence guaranteed to them. We are giving them what they never could have got with their own strength, what they could have got only by the united strength of the armies of the world. When we had determined the boundaries of Poland we set it up and recognized it as an independent Republic. Poland never could have freed herself. There is a Minister, a diplomatic representative, of the United States at Warsaw right now in virtue of our formal recognition of the Republic of Poland.

But upon Poland center some of the dangers of the future. South of Poland is Bohemia, in all her veins the strongest national impulse that was to be found anywhere in Europe, which we cut away from the Austrian combination. Below Bohemia is Hungary which can no longer rely upon the assistant strength of Austria; below her is an enlarged Roumania. Alongside of Roumania is the new Slavic Kingdom, that never could have won its own independence, which had chafed under the chains of Austria-Hungary, but never could throw them off. When strategic claims were urged, it was matter of common counsel that such considerations were not in our thought; we were not arranging for future wars—we were giving people what belonged to them. We said, "The fundamental wrongs of history center in those regions. These people have the right to govern their own government and control their own fortunes."

Now the world is waiting to hear whether the United States will join in doing for them what it sanely did for Cuba, guaranteeing their freedom and saying to them, "What we have given to you no man shall take away." It is our final heroic test of character, and I, for one, have not the slightest doubt as to what the result of the test is going to be, because I know that at heart this people loves freedom and right and justice more than it loves money and material prosperity or any of the things that anybody can get but nobody can keep unless they have elevation of spirit enough to see the horizons of the destiny of man. When we came into existence as a nation we promised ourselves and we promised the world that we would serve liberty everywhere. We were only 3,000,000 strong then, and shall we, when more than a hundred million strong, fail to fulfill the promise that we made when we were weak? We have served mankind and we shall continue to serve mankind, for I believe that we are the flower of mankind so far as civilization is concerned.

CARING FOR WEAK NATIONS

I hear some gentlemen say, "Ah! but that is altruistic. It is not our business to take care of the weak nations of the world." No, but it is our business to prevent war, and if we do not take care of the weak nations of the world, there will be war. These gentlemen assume the role of being very practical men, and they say, "We do not want to get into war to protect every little nation in the world." Very well then, let them show me how they will keep out of war by not protecting them, and let them show me how they will prove that having gone into an enterprise, they are not absolute contemptible quitters if they do not see the game through. They joined with the rest of us in the profession of fine purpose when we went into the war, and what was the fine purpose that we professed? They went in, and they professed to go in, to see to it that nobody after Germany's defeat should repeat the experiment which Germany had tried. And how do they propose to do that? To leave the material that Germany was going to make her dominating empire out of, helpless and at her mercy. You cannot set weak peoples up in independence and then leave them to be preyed upon. You cannot give a false gift. You cannot give to people rights which they never enjoyed before and say, "Now, keep them if you can." That is an Indian gift. That is a gift which cannot be kept. If you have a really humane purpose and a real knowledge of the conditions of peace in the world, you will have to say, "This is the settlement and we guarantee its continuance."

There is only one honorable course when

you have won a cause, to see that it stays won
and nobody interferes with or disturbs the
results. We have not made them strong by
making them independent. We have given
them what I have called their land title. By
giving them their land titles you do not make
them any stronger. You make them stronger
in spirit; it may be they see a new day, they
feel a new enthusiasm, their old love of their
country can now express itself in action, but
physically they are no stronger than they
were before, and that road that we heard so
much of—from Bremen to Bagdad—is wide
open. New States, one after another, have
been set up by the action of the conference at
Paris all along the route that was intended to
be the route of German dominion, and if we
now merely set them up and leave them in
their weakness to take care of themselves,
then Germans can at their leisure, by intriguing, by every subtle process of which they are
master, accomplish what they could not accomplish by arms, and we will have abandoned
the people whom we redeemed. The thing is
inconceivable; the thing is impossible. If you
leave that road open, if you leave those nations to take care of themselves, then you have
committed the unpardonable sin of undoing
the victory which our boys won. If the results
of this liberation are not guaranteed, then

they will fall down like a house of cards. You cannot establish freedom without force, and the only force you can substitute for an armed mankind is the concerted force of the combined action of mankind through the instrumentality of all the enlightened governments of the world. This is the only conceivable system that you can substitute for the old order of things which brought the calamity of this war upon us and would assuredly bring the calamity of another war upon us. If we leave them there without the guaranty that the combined force of the world will assure their independence and their territorial integrity, we have only to wait a short generation when our recent experience will be repeated. We did not let Germany dominate the world this time. Are we then?

That guaranty is the only guarantee against the repetition of the war we have gone through just as soon as the German nation, 60,000,000 strong, can again recover its strength and its spirit, for east of Germany lies the fertile field of intrigue and power. There is no conjecture about this. Is there any man who does not know that the seed of war in the modern world is industrial and commercial rivalry? The real reason that the war we have just finished took place was that Germany was afraid her commercial rivals were going to get the better of her; and the reason why some nations went into the war against Germany was that they thought Germany would get the commercial advantage of them. This war in its inception was a commercial and industrial war. It was not a political war. The seed of the jealousy, the seed of the deep-seated hatred, was hot, successful commercial and industrial rivalry. The rivalries of this war have not cooled. The passions of this world are not dead. They have been rendered hotter than ever. We know the former purposes of German intrigue in this country, and they are being revived. Why?

We have not reduced very materially the number of the German people. Germany remains the great power of Central Europe. She has more than 60,000,000 people now (she had nearly 70,000,000 before Poland and other Provinces were taken away). You cannot change the temper and expectations of a people by five years of war, particularly five years of war in which they are not yet conscious of the wrong they did or of the wrong way in which they did it. They are expecting the time of the revival of their power, and along with the revival of their power goes their extraordinary capacity, their unparalleled education, their great capacity in commerce and finance and manufacture.

At this moment, the only people who are dealing with the Bolshevist Government in Russia are the Germans. They are fraternizing with the few who exercise control in that distracted country. They are making all their plans that the financing of Russia and the commerce of Russia and the development of Russia shall be as soon as possible in the hands of the Germans; and just as soon as she can swing that great power, that is also her road to the East and to the domination of the world.

WORLD IN REVOLUTION

What does not seem to me realized in this blessed country of ours is the fact that the world is in revolution. I do not mean in active revolution. I do not mean that it is in a state of mind that will bring about the dissolution of governments. I mean that it is in a state of mind which may bring about the dissolution of governments if we do not enter into a world settlement which will really in fact and in power establish justice and right. In every part of the world, not excluding our own beloved country, there are men who feel that society has been shaken to its foundations, and that it ought to have been shaken to its foundations, in order that men might be awakened to the wrongs that had been done

[164]

and were continuing to be done. There is unrest all over the world. The unrest is not due merely to the fact of recent extraordinary circumstances.

There is not now a country in the world where the great mass of mankind is not aware of its rights and determined to have them at any cost, and the present universal unrest in the world, which renders return to normal conditions impossible, so long as it continues, will not stop until men are assured by some arrangement they can believe in that their rights will be protected and that they can go about the normal production of the necessaries of life and begin to enjoy the extraordinary pleasures and privileges of life without the constant shadow of some cloud of terror over them, some threat of injustice, some tyranny of control. It is due to a universal conviction that the conditions under which men live and labor are unsatisfactory. It is a conviction all over the world that there is no use talking about political democracy unless you have also industrial democracy.

You know what this war interrupted in the United States. We were looking closely at our own methods of doing business. A great many were convinced that the control of the business of this country was in too few hands. Some were convinced that the control of the credit of the country was in too few hands. Some were convinced that the control of the credit of the country was controlled by small groups of men, and the great Federal Reserve Act and the Great Land Bank Act were passed in order to release the resources of the country on a broader and more generous scale. We had not finished dealing with monopolies. We have not finished dealing with monopolies. With monopolies there can be no industrial democracy. With the control of the few, of whatever kind or class, there can be no democracy of any sort. The world is finding that out in some portions of it in blood and terror.

THE LESSON OF RUSSIA

Look what has happened in Russia. I find wherever I go in America that my fellow citizens feel as I do, an infinite pity for that great people, an infinite longing to be of some service to them. Everybody who has mixed with the Russian people tells me that they are among the most lovable people in the world, a very gentle people, a very friendly people, a very simple people, and in their local life a very democratic people who easily trust you and who expect you to be trustworthy as they are.

I wish we could learn the lesson of Russia so that it would be burned into the consciousness of every man and woman in America. That lesson is that nobody can be free where there is not public order and authority. What has happened in Russia is that an old and distinguished and skillful autocracy has had put in its place an amateur autocracy. What happened in Russia was not a sudden and accidental thing. The people of Russia were maddened with the suppression of Czarism. When at last the time came to throw off those chains, they threw them off, at first with hearts full of confidence and hope, and then they found out that they had been again deceived. There was an assembly chosen to frame a constitution for them and it was suppressed and dispersed, and a little group of men just as selfish, just as ruthless, just as pitiless as the agents of the Czar himself, assumed control and exercised their power by terror and not by right.

We ourselves are in danger at this present moment of minorities trying to control our affairs, and whenever a minority tries to control the affairs of the country it is fighting against the interests of the country just as much as if it were trying to upset the government. I am against the control of any minority anywhere. Search your own economic history and what have you been uneasy about? Now and again you have said that there were small groups of capitalists who were controlling the industry and therefore the development of the United States. If that is so, and sometimes I have feared that it was, we must break up that monopoly. I am not now saying that there is any group of our fellow citizens who are consciously doing anything of the kind. I am saying that these allegations must be proved, but if it is proved that any class, any group anywhere, is without the suffrage of their fellow citizens, in control of our affairs, then I am with you to destroy the power of that group. We have got to be frank with ourselves however; if we do not want minority government in Russia, we must see that we do not have it in the United States. If you do not want little groups of selfish men to plot the future of Europe, we must not allow little groups of selfish men to plot the future of America. That picture is before the eyes of every nation. Shall we get into the clutch of another sort of minority? Any man that speaks for a class must prove that he also speaks for all his fellow citizens and for mankind, and then we will listen to him. The most difficult thing in a democracy is to get classes where they unfortunately exist to understand one another and unite, and yet you have not got a great democracy until they do understand one another and unite. So that if we are in for seeing that there are no more

Czars, and no more Kaisers, then let us do a thorough job and see that nothing of that sort occurs anywhere. That is what pitiful Russia has got in for, and there will be many a year, I am afraid, before she finds herself again.

Have you seen no symptoms of the spread of that sort of chaotic spirit into other countries? That poison is running through the veins of the world, and we have made the methods of communication throughout the world such that all the veins of the world are open and the poison can circulate. Do you not know that the world is all now one single whispering gallery? Those antennæ of the wireless telegraph are the symbols of our age. All the impulses of mankind are thrown out upon the air and reach to the ends of the earth; quietly upon steamships, silently under the cover of the Postal Service, with the tongue of the wireless, and the tongue of the telegraph, all the suggestions of disorder are spread through the world. The dread in the mind of every thoughtful man in Europe is that that distemper will spread to their countries, and that before there will be settled order there will be tragical disorder. There is not a statesman in Europe who does not dread the infection of it, and just as certainly as those people are disconcerted, thrown back upon their own resources, disheartened, rendered cynical by the withdrawal of the only people in the world they trust, just so certainly there will be universal upsetting of order in Europe; and if the order of Europe is upset, do you think America is going to be quiet?

Have you heard nothing of the propaganda of that sort of belief in the United States? Does any body of Americans think that none of this restlessness, this unhappy feeling, has reached America? Are our affairs entirely in order? Do you find everybody about you content with our present industrial order? Do you hear of no intimations of radical change? Do you learn of no organizations, the object of which is nothing less than to overturn the government itself? There is only one way to meet radicalism and that is to deprive it of food, and wherever there is anything wrong there is abundant food for radicalism. The only way to keep men from agitating against grievances is to remove the grievances, and as long as things are wrong I do not intend to ask men to stop agitating. I intend to beg that they will agitate in an orderly fashion; I intend to beg that they will use the orderly methods of counsel, and, it may be, the slow processes of correction which can be accomplished in a self-governing people through political means. Otherwise we will have chaos; but as long as there is something to correct, I say Godspeed to the men who are trying to correct it. That is the only way to meet radicalism. Radicalism means cutting up by the roots. Well remove the noxious growth and there will be no cutting up by the roots. We are a self-possessed nation. We know the value of order. We mean to maintain it. We will not permit any minority of any sort to dominate it, but it is rather important for America as well as for the rest of the world, that this infection should not be everywhere in the air, and that men everywhere should begin to look life and facts in the face and come to calm counsels and purposes that will bring order and happiness and prosperity again.

OUR PRESENT TASKS

The tasks of peace that are ahead of us are the most difficult to which the human genius has ever been devoted. We have to re-regulate the fortunes of men. We have to reconstruct the machinery of civilization. I use the words deliberately—we have to reconstruct the machinery of civilization.

The problem that we are facing in the high cost of living is the end and the beginning and a portion of a world problem, and the great difficulty just now is in getting some minds adjusted to the world. One of the difficulties that are being encountered is not prejudice so much but that thing which is so common and so inconvenient—just downright ignorance. Ignorance, I mean, of the state of the world and of America's relation to the state of the world. We cannot change that relation. It is a fact. It is a fact bigger than anybody of us, and one of the advantages that the United States has it ought not to forfeit: it is made up out of all the thinking peoples of the world. We come from all the great races of the world. We are made up out of all the nations and peoples who have stood at the center of civilization.

Sometimes I feel like taking off my hat to some of those immigrants. I was born an American. I could not help it, but they chose to be, Americans. I honor those men. I say, "You made a deliberate choice which showed that you saw what the drift and history of mankind was." We are made up out of the hard-headed, hard-fisted, practical and yet idealistic and forward-looking peoples of the world, and we, of all peoples, ought to have an international understanding and ability to comprehend what the problem is and what part we ought to play in that problem.

Every other nation is set in the mold of a particular breeding. We are set in no mold at

all. Every other nation has certain preposses-
sions which run back through all the ramifi-
cations of an ancient history. We have nothing of the kind. This nation draws its blood
from every civilized stock in the world and is
ready by sympathy and understanding to
understand the peoples of the world, their interests, their rights, their hopes, their destiny.
America is the only nation in the world that
has that equipment. We are the people of all
people in the world intelligently to discuss the
difficulties of the nations which we represent,
although we are Americans. We are the pre-
destined mediators of mankind. I am not saying this in any kind of national pride or van-
ity. I believe it is mere historic truth, and I
try to interpret circumstances in some intelli-
gent way. If that is the kind of people we are,
it must have been intended that we should
make some use of the opportunities and powers that we have.

I hear men say, "Let us stay out and take
care of ourselves and let the rest of the world
take care of itself. Why should we rehabilitate
the world?" I do not agree with that from the
point of view of sentiment. I would be ashamed to agree with it from the point of view
of sentiment, and I think I have intelligence
enough to know that it would not work, even
if I wanted it to work.

OUR FOREIGN TRADE

Are we disconnected from the rest of the world? Take a single item. If Europe is disordered, who is going to buy wheat? There is more wheat in this country than we can consume. There are more foodstuffs in this country of many sorts than we can consume. Who is going to change the circumstance that we largely feed the rest of the world? Who is going to check the growth of this nation? Who is going to reduce the natural resources of this country? Who is going to change the circumstance that many of our resources are unique and indispensable? If you want to trade you have got to have somebody to trade with. If you want to carry your business to the ends of the world, there must be business at the ends of the world to tie in with. You cannot trade with a world disordered. What are you going to do? Give up your foreign markets? The 300,000,000 people between the Rhine and the Ural Mountains will be in such a condition that they cannot buy anything, their industries cannot start, unless they surrender themselves to the bankers of Mittel-Europa, that you used to hear about; and the peoples of Italy and France and Belgium, some 80,-000,000 strong, who are your natural customers, cannot buy anything in disturbed and bankrupt Europe. You cannot get those markets away from Germany if you let her reestablish her old influence there.

I believe that with the exception of the United States, there is not a country in the world that can live without importation. There are only one or two countries that can live without imported foodstuffs. There is hardly an European nation that is of a fighting inclination, which has enough food to eat without importing food. There are no countries that I know of that can live in their ordinary way without importing manufactured goods or raw materials, raw materials of many kinds. Is there any business man who would be willing to see the world go bankrupt and the business of the world stop? Is there any man who does not know that America is the only nation left by the war in a position to see that the world does go on with its business? I dare say you read the statement of Mr. Herbert Hoover's opinion, an opinion which I always greatly respect, that it will be necessary for the United States to advance four or five billion dollars for the rehabilitation of credit and industry on the other side of the water. I think the statement of the sum a reasonable and conservative statement. If we do not start the world again, then we check and stop to that extent our own industries and our own exportation, of course. If you want to have your own fortunes held steady, realize that the fortunes of the world must be held steady. If the business of the world lags your industries lag and your prosperity lags.

REHABILITATION OF GERMANY

What is our own business? We are a great nation but the Treaty is going to be applied just the same whether we take part in it or not. What is one of the central features of the execution of this Treaty? It is the application of the reparation clauses. Germany cannot pay for this war unless her industries are revived, and the Treaty of Peace sets up a great commission known as the Reparation Commission, in which it was intended that there hould be a member from the United States is well as from other countries. The business of this Commission will be in part to see that the industries of Germany are revived in order that Germany may pay this great debt which she owes to civilization. Not only that, but you know we used to have a trade with Germany. All of that trade is going to be in the hands and under the control of the Reparation Commission. I humbly asked leave to appoint a member to look after our interests, and I was rebuked for it. I am looking after the industrial relations of the United States. I would like to see the other men who are. They are forgetting the industrial interests of the United States, and they are doing things that will cut us off and our trade off from the normal channels, because the Reparation Commission can determine where Germany buys, what Germany buys, how much Germany buys; the Reparation Commission can determine in what instruments of credit she temporally expresses her debt. They can determine how those instruments of credit shall be used for the basis of the credit which must underlie international exchange. They are going to stand at the center of the financial operations of the world. Now, is it minding our business to keep out of that? On the contrary, it is handing our business over to people who are not particularly interested in seeing that it prospers. At every point we shall be embarrassed by the whole financial affairs of the world being in the hands of other nations.

I do not like, in debating the great traditions of a free people, to bring the debate down to the basis of dollars and cents, but if you want to bring it down to that, if anybody wants to bring it down to that, reason it out on that line. If you want, as some of our fellow countrymen insist, to dwell upon the material side of it and our interest in the matter, our commercial interest, draw the picture for yourselves. The strain put upon the finances of the other governments of the world has been all but a breaking strain. I imagine that it will be several generations before foreign governments can finally adjust themselves to carrying the overwhelming debts which have been accumulated in this war. The United States has accumulated a great debt but not in proportion to those that other countries have accumulated when you reckon our wealth as compared with theirs. We are the only nation in the world that is likely, in the immediate future, to have a sufficient body of free capital to put the industrial world here and elsewhere on its feet again. I have heard Europe spoken of as bankrupt. There may be great difficulties in paying the public debts, but there are going to be no insuperable difficulties to re-beginning the economic and industrial life of Europe. The men are there, the materials are there, the energy is there, and the hope is there. The nations are not crushed. They are ready for the great enterprises of the future, and it is for us to choose whether we will enter those great enterprises upon a footing of advantage and of honor or upon a footing of disadvantage and distrust.

The other nations of the world are drawing together. We, who suggested that they should draw together in this new partnership, stand aside. We at once draw their suspicion upon us. We at once draw their intense hostility upon us. We at once renew the thing that had begun to be done before we went into the war. There was a conference in Paris not many months before we went into the war in which the nations then engaged against Germany attempted to draw together in an exclusive economic combination where they should serve one another's interest and exclude those who had not participated in the war from sharing in that interest, and just so certainly as we stay out, every market that can possibly be closed against us will be closed. If you merely look at it from the point of view of the material prosperity of the United States, we are under compulsion to stay in the partnership. You cannot have even your legitimate part in the business of the world unless you are partners with the rest. Is it your idea that if we lend our money, as we must, to men whom we have bitterly disappointed, that money will bring back to us the largess to which we are entitled? Can you sell more easily to a man who takes your goods because he cannot do without them or to a man who wants them and believes them the best?

We are told that we are strong and they are weak; that we still have economic independence and they have not. What does that mean? That means that they went into the redemption of the freedom of the world sooner than we did and gave everything that they had to redeem it; and now we, because we did not go in so soon or lose so much, want to make profit of the redeemers! The thing is hideous. The thing is unworthy of every tradition of America. I speak of it not because I think that sort of thing takes the least hold upon the consciousness or the purpose of America, but because it is a pleasure to condemn so ugly a thing. There is nothing which can more certainly put a drop of acid into every relationship we have in the world than if we now desert our former associates in the war.

You can bring about a state of mind whereby every device possible, foreign markets will be closed to you and men will say, "No, the wheat of America tastes bitter; we will eat the wheat of Argentina; we will eat the wheat of Australia, for that is the wheat of friendship, and this is the wheat of antagonism. We do not want to wear clothes made out of American cotton: we are going to buy just as much cotton from India as we can. We are going to develop new cotton fields. America is up to something: we do not know just what, and we are going to shut and lock every door against her." You can get the world in that temper.

Do you think it would be profitable? You make all the lines of trade lines of resistance unless you prove true to the things that you have attempted and undertaken. Unless you go into the great economic partnership with the world, you have the rest of the world economically combined against you. If we are partners, let me predict we will be the senior partner. The financial leadership will be ours. The industrial primacy will be ours. The commercial advantage will be ours. If we are in it, then we are going to be the determining factor in the development of civilization. If we are out of it, we ourselves are going to watch every other nation with suspicion, and we will be justified, too; and we are going to be watched with suspicion. Every movement of trade, every relationship of manufacture, every question of raw materials, every matter that affects the intercourse of the world will be impeded by the consciousness that America wants to hold off and get something which she is not willing to share with the rest of mankind.

AMERICA'S OPPORTUNITY

Only those ignorant of the world can believe that any nation, even so great a nation as the United States, can stand alone and play a single part in the history of mankind. The facts of the world have changed. We have managed in the process of civilization, to make a world that cannot be taken to pieces. The pieces are dove-tailed and intimately fitted with one another, and unless you assemble them as you do the intimate parts of a great machine, civilization will not work. We are tied into the rest of the world by kinship, by sympathy, by interest in every great enterprise of human affairs. The United States has become the economic center of the world, the financial center. Our advice is constantly sought. Our economic engagements run everywhere, into every part of the globe. Our assistance is essential to the establishment of normal conditions throughout the world. You can no more separate yourselves from the rest of the world than you can take all the tender roots of a great tree out of the earth and expect the tree to live. All the tendrils of our life, economic and social and every other, are interlaced in a way that is inextricable with the similar tendrils of the rest of mankind. Shall we exercise our influence in the world, which can henceforth be a profound and controlling influence, at a great advantage or at an insuperable disadvantage?

We are not the only people who have made up our mind that our government must devote its attention to peace and justice, and to right. The people all over the world have made up their minds to that. Political liberty can exist only when there is peace. What kind of peace are we going to have and what kind of guaranties are there to be behind that peace? That is what is concerning me. I know the splendid steadiness of the American people, but the whole world needs that steadiness, and the American people are the makeweight in the fortunes of mankind. How long are we going to debate into which scale we will throw that magnificent equipoise that belongs to us? How long shall we be kept waiting for the answer whether the world may trust us or despise us? They have looked to us for leadership. They have looked to us for example. They have built their peace upon the basis of our suggestions. That great volume that contains the Treaty of Peace is drawn along the specifications laid down by the American Government, and now the world stands at amaze because an authority in America hesitates whether it will endorse an American document or not. The world is waiting, waiting to see, not whether we will take part but whether we will serve and lead, for it has expected us to lead. Shall we falter at the very critical moment when we are finally to write our name to the standing pledge which we then took?

I want to remind you that many other nations were put under a deeper temptation than we. Belgium did not hesitate to underwrite civilization. It would have been possible for little Belgium at any time to make terms with the enemy. Belgium was not prepared to resist. Belgium knew that resistance was useless. Belgium knew that she could get any term of advantage from Germany she pleased, if she would only submit, and at the cost of everything that she had Belgium did nothing less than underwrite civilization. I do not know anywhere in history a more inspiring fact than that.

Italy could have had her terms with Austria at almost any period of the war, particularly just before she made her final stand at the Piave River, but she would not compound with the enemy. She, too, had underwritten civilization. She also was a trustee for civilization, and she would not sell the birthright of mankind for any sort of material advantage.

And Serbia, the first of the helpless nations to be struck down, her armies driven from her own soil, maintained her armies on other soil. The armies of Serbia were never dispersed. Whether they could be on their own soil or not, they were fighting for their rights and through their rights for the rights of civilized man.

AMERICA AND WORLD PROBLEMS

I believe that America is going to be more willing than any other nation in the world, when it gets its voice heard, to do the same thing that these little nations did. I believe in my heart that there is hardly a man in America, if you get really back of his superficial thoughts, who is not man enough to be willing to make the sacrifice to underwrite civilization. It is only sacrifice that tells. Don't you remember what we used to cry during the Liberty Loans, "Lend until it hurts." Now that the great Treaty of Peace has established the oppressed peoples of the world who are affected by this Treaty on their own territory, given them their own freedom, given them command of their own affairs, they are looking to America to show them how to use that new liberty and that new power.

WHY AMERICAN ISOLATION IS IMPOSSIBLE

When men tell you that we are, by going into the League of Nations, reversing the policy of the United States, they have not thought the thing out. The statement is not true. It is impossible for the United States to be isolated. The isolation of the United States is at an end, not because we chose to go into the politics of the world but because by the sheer genius of this people and the growth of our power we have become a determining fac-

tor in the history of mankind, and after you
have become a determining factor you cannot
remain isolated, whether you want to or not.
America is going to grow more and more powerful and the more powerful she is the more inevitable it is that she should be the trustee for
the peace of the world. I am not stating it as
a matter of power. I am not stating it with the
thought that the United States has greater
material wealth and greater physical power
than any other nation. The point that I want
you to get is a very profound point; the point
is that the United States is the only nation in
the world that has sufficient moral force with
the rest of the world. While old rivalries and
old jealousies and many of the intricate
threads of history woven in unhappy patterns
have made the rest of the world suspect one
another nobody doubts America. It is the
only nation that has proved its disinterestedness. It is the only nation which is not suspected by the other nations of the world of
ulterior purposes. There is not a Province in
Europe in which American troops would not
at this moment be welcomed with open arms,
because the population would know that they
had come as friends and would go as soon as
their errand was fulfilled. That is the reputation of American soldiers throughout Europe,
and it is their reputation because it is true.

That is the temper in which they go; that is
the principle upon which they act and upon
which the government back of them acts, and
the great people whom that government represents. What an extraordinary tribute to the
principles of the United States! What an extraordinary tribute to the sincerity of the people of the United States! America is the only
nation whose guarantee will suffice to substitute discussion for war. And all the world,
provided we do not betray them by rejecting
this Treaty, will continue to regard us as their
friends and follow us as their friends and serve
us as their friends. It is the noblest opportunity ever offered to a great people.

You have been told that Washington advised us against entangling alliances, and gentlemen have used that as an argument against
the League of Nations. What Washington had
in mind was exactly what these gentlemen
want to lead us back to. The day we have left
behind us was a day of alliances. It was a day
of balances of power. It was a day of "every
nation take care of itself or make a partnership with some other nation or group of nations to hold the peace of the world steady or
to dominate the weaker portions of the world."
Those were the days of alliances. This project
of the League of Nations is a great process of
disentanglement. The people of the world are

tired of every other kind of experiment except the one we are going to try. I have called it an experiment; I frankly admit that it is an experiment, but it is a very promising experiment, because there is not a statesman in the world who does not know that his people demand it. The world has turned a corner that it will never turn again. The old order is gone and nobody can build it up again.

OPPONENTS HAVE NO PLAN

I want you to realize those Americans who are opposing this plan of a League of Nations offer no substitute. There is a great constructive plan presented, and no man in the presence of the present critical situation of mankind has the right to oppose any constructive plan except by a better constructive plan. If anybody dares to defeat this great experiment, then he must gather together the counsellors of the world and do something better. If there is a better scheme, I for one will subscribe to it. A great plan is the only thing that can defeat a great plan. They offer nothing that they pretend will accomplish the same object. The only thing that wins against a program is a better program. They are ready to go back to that old and ugly plan of armed nations, of alliances, of watchful jealousies, of rabid antagonisms, of purposes concealed, running by the subtle channels of intrigue through the veins of people who do not dream what poison is being injected into their systems.

Now are we going to bring about a peace for which everything waits? We cannot bring it about by doing nothing! America cannot bring about peace by herself. No other nation can bring about peace by itself. The agreement of a small group of nations cannot bring about peace. The peace of the world cannot be established without America. America is necessary to the peace of the world. And reverse the proposition: The peace and goodwill of the world are necessary to America. I have been very much amazed and very much amused, if I could be amused in such critical circumstances, to see that the statesmanship of some gentlemen consists in the very interesting proposition that we do nothing at all. I had heard of standing pat before, but I never had heard before of standpatism going to the length of saying it is none of our business and we do not care what happens to the rest of the world. Negation will not serve the world. Generalities will not penetrate to the heart of this great question. Let me pay the tribute which it is only just that I should pay to some of the men who have been, I believe, misunderstood in this business. It is only a handful of men who are trying to defeat the Treaty or to prevent the League. The great majority, in official bodies and out, are scrutinizing it, as it is perfectly legitimate that they should scrutinize it, to see if it is necessary that they should qualify it in any respect, and my knowledge of their conscience, my knowledge of their public principle, makes me certain that they will sooner or later see that it is safest since it is all expressed in the plainest English that the English dictionary affords, not to qualify it—to accept it as it is. They cannot in conscience or good faith deprive us of this great work of peace without substituting some other that is better. Qualified adoption is not adoption. Qualification means asking special exemptions and privileges for the United States. We cannot ask that. Negations are not going to construct the policies of mankind. The world cannot breathe in an atmosphere of negations. The world cannot deal with nations who say, "We wont play." The world cannot have anything to do with an arrangement in which every nation says, "We will take care of ourselves." Opposition is not going to save the world. Opposition constructs nothing. Opposition is the specialty of those who are Bolshevistically inclined—and again I assure you I am not comparing any of my respected colleagues to Bolshevists; I am merely pointing out that the Bolshevist spirit lacks every element of constructiveness. They have destroyed everything and they propose nothing, and while there is a common abhorrence for political Bolshevism, I hope there will not be such a thing growing up in our country as international Bolshevism, the Bolshevism which destroys the constructive work of men who have conscientiously tried to cement the good feeling of the great peoples of the world.

I have feared at times that there were those amongst us who did not realize just what the heart of this question is. I have been afraid that their thoughts were lingering in a past day when the calculation was always of national advantage, and that it had not come to see the light of the new day in which men are thinking of the common advantage and safety of mankind. The issue is nothing else. Either we must stand apart, and in the phrase of some gentlemen, "take care of ourselves," which means antagonize others, or we must join hands with the other great nations of the world and with the weak nations of the world, in seeking that justice is everywhere maintained. You know you cannot establish civil society if anybody is going to be a neutral with regard to the maintenance of the law. We are all bound in conscience, and all public officers are bound in oath, not to remain neutral with regard to the maintenance of the law and the vindication of the right, and one of the things that occurred in this conference, was this: One of the principles that I went to Paris most insisting on was the freedom of the seas. Now, the freedom of the seas means the definition of the right of neutrals to use the seas when other nations are at war, but under the League of Nations there are no neutrals, and, therefore, what I have called the practical joke on myself was that by the very thing that I was advocating it became unnecessary to define the freedom of the seas. All nations are engaged to maintain the right, and in that sense no nation can be neutral when the right is invaded, and, all being comrades and partners in a common cause, we all have an equal right to use the seas. To my mind it is a much better solution than had occurred to me, or than had occurred to anyone else with regard to that single definition of right. We must go forward with this concert of nations or we must go back to the old arrangement, because the guaranties of peace will not be sufficient without the United States, and those who oppose this Covenant are driven to the necessity of advocating the old order of balances of power. If you do not have this universal concert, you have what we have always avoided, necessary alignment of this or that nation with one other nation or with some other group of nations.

OPPOSITION HELPS GERMANY

What is disturbing me most about the present debate—not because I doubt its issue, but because I regret its length—is that it is heartening the representatives of Germany to believe that at last they are going to do in this way what they were not able to do by arms, separate us in interest and purpose from our associates in the war. The League of Nations is very near the heart of the people. There are some men in public life who do not seem to be in touch with the heart of the people, but those who are know how that heart throbs deep and strong for this great enterprise of humanity, for it is nothing less than that. We must set our purposes in a very definite way to assist the judgment of public men. I do not mean in any way to coerce the judgment of public men, but to enlighten and assist that judgment, for I am convinced, after crossing the continent, that there is no sort of doubt that 80 per cent of the people of the United States are for the League of Nations, and that the chief opposition outside legislative halls comes from the very disquieting element that we had to deal with before and during the war. All the elements that tended toward disloyalty are against the League and for a very good reason. If this is not adopted we will serve Germany's purpose, because we will be dissociated from the nations, and I am afraid permanently dissociated from the nations with whom we cooperated in defeating Germany.

I am not suggesting, I have no right to suggest, that the men who are opposing this Covenant have any thought of assisting Germany in their minds, but my point is that by doing what they are doing they are assisting Germany, whether they want to do so or not. I would not have you understand me to mean that the men who are opposing the ratification of the Treaty are consciously encouraging the pro-German propaganda. I have no right to say that or to think it, but I do say that what they are doing is encouraging the pro-German propaganda, and that it is bringing about a hope in the minds of those whom we have just spent our precious blood to defeat that they may separate us from the rest of the world and produce this interesting spectacle, only two nations standing aside from this great concert and guaranty of peace—beaten Germany and triumphant America. No part of the world has been so pleased by our present hesitation as the leaders of Germany, because their hope from the first has been that sooner or later we would fall out with our associates. Their hope was to divide us before the fighting stopped, and now their hope is to divide us after the fighting.

America is necessary to the peace of the world. Germany realizes it; and Germany wants us to stay out of this Treaty. Not under any deception. Not under the deception that we will turn in sympathy toward her. Not under the delusion that we would seek in any direct or conscious way to serve Germany, but with the knowledge that the guaranties will not be sufficient without America, and that, inasmuch as Germany is out of the arrangement, it will be very useful to Germany to have America out of the arrangement. The things prescribed in this Treaty will not be fully carried out if anyone of the great influences that brought that result about is withheld from its consummation. Germany knows that if America is out of the arrangement America will lose the confidence and cooperation of all the other nations in the world, and, fearing America's strength, she wants to see America alienated from the peoples from whom she has been alienated. It is a perfectly reasonable program. She wants to see America isolated. She desires nothing so much as that we should be isolated, because she knows that then the same kind of suspicion, the same kind of hostility, the same kind of unfriendliness—that subtle poison that brings every trouble that comes between nations—will center on the United States as well as upon Germany. She is isolated. Her isolation will be broken; she will have a comrade, whether that nation wants to be her comrade or not, and what the lads did on the fields of France will be undone. She wants to see one great nation left out of the combination which she never would dare face again. I want those who have any kind of sympathy for the purposes with which we went into the war now to reflect upon this proposition: Are we going to prove the enemy of the rest of the world just when we have proved its savior? It would touch the honor of the United States very near if at the end of this great struggle we should seek to take the position which our enemies desire and our friends deplore.

INSURANCE AGAINST WAR

Men have asked me, "Do you think that the League of Nations is an absolute guarantee against war?" Of course it is not. Nobody in his senses claims for the Covenant of the League of Nations that it is certain to stop war. Senator Lodge says if we can stop some wars it is worth while. No human arrangement can give you an absolute guarantee against human passion, but I answer that

question with another, If it only creates a presumption that there will not be war, would
you not rather have that presumption than
live under the certainty that there will be
war? Though the chance should be poor, is it
not worth taking a chance? Let men discount
the proposed arrangements as much as they
will; let us regard it as an insurance policy. If
you thought you had fifty per cent insurance
against war, would you not jump at it? If you
thought you had thirty per cent insurance
against war, would you not take it? If you
thought you had ten per cent insurance, would
you not think it better than nothing? If you
can get a little insurance against an infinite
catastrophe, is it not better than getting none
at all? If the nations of the world will indeed
and in truth accept this great Covenant of a
League of Nations and agree to put arbitration and discussion always first and war always last, I say that we have an immense insurance against war, and that is exactly what
this great Covenant does. I take it you want
some insurance against war rather than none,
and the experience of the world demonstrates
that this is an almost complete insurance. The
one thing that a wrong cause cannot stand is
exposure. The best way to dissipate nonsense
is to expose it to the open air. The particular
thing in the Covenant of the League of Na-

tions is that every cause shall be deliberately exposed to the judgment of mankind. It substitutes what the whole world has long been for, namely, arbitration and discussion for war. In other words, all the great fighting nations of the world—for Germany for the time being, at any rate, is not a great fighting nation—promise to lay their case, whatever it may be, before the whole jury of humanity. They put it either before a jury by whom they are bound or before a jury which will publish all the facts to mankind and express a frank opinion regarding it. You have here what the world must have, what America went into this war to obtain. You have here an estoppel of the brutal sudden impulse of war. You have here a restraint upon the passions of ambitious nations. If there had been any arrangement comparable with this in 1914, the calamitous war which we have just passed through would have been inconceivable. There is no other way to do it than by a universal league of nations, and what is proposed is a universal league of nations.

The majestic thing about the League of Nations is that it is to include the great peoples of the world, all except Germany. Germany is one of the great peoples of the world. I would be ashamed not to say that. Those 60,000,000 industrious and inventive and accomplished

people are one of the great peoples of the
world. They have been put upon. They have
been misled. Their minds have been debased
by a false philosophy. They have been taught
things that the human spirit ought to reject,
but they will come out of that nightmare,
they will come out of that phantasm, and they
will again be a great people. And when they
are out of it, when they have got over that
dream of conquest and of oppression, when
they have shown that their government really
is based upon new principles and upon democratic principles, then we, all of us at Paris
agree that they should be admitted to the
League of Nations.

In order to meet the present situation, we
have got to know what we are dealing with.
Look at this thing in a new aspect, look upon
it not with calculations of interest, not with
fear of responsibility, but with a consciousness of the great moral issue which the United
States must now decide. We are not dealing
with the kind of document which this is represented by some gentlemen to be, and inasmuch as we are dealing with a document simon
pure in respect of the very principles we have
professed to live up to, we have got to do one
or other of two things, we have either got to
adopt it or reject it. I say without qualification that every nation that is not afraid of

the judgment of mankind will go into this arrangement. There is nothing for any nation to lose whose purposes are right and whose cause is just. The only nations that need fear to go into it are those that have designs that are inconsistent with justice and are the opposite of peace. The issue is final. We cannot avoid it. We either go in with the other free peoples of the world to guarantee the peace of the world now, or we stay out and on some dark and disastrous day we seek admission to the League of Nations along with Germany. If we keep out of this League now, we can never enter it except alongside of Germany. We either go in now or come in later with our recent enemies. Every great fighting nation in the world is on the list of those who are to constitute the League of Nations. I say every great nation, because America is going to be included among them, and the only choice is whether we will go in now or come in later with Germany; whether we will go in as founders of this covenant of freedom or go in as those who are admitted after they have made a mistake and repented. If you are going to put into the world American enterprise and American faith and American vision, then you must be the principal partners in the new partnership which the world is forming. I take it you are too proud to ask to be exempted from responsibilities which the other members of the League will carry. We go in upon equal terms or we do not go in at all; and if we do not go in, think of the tragedy of that result, the only sufficient guaranty of the peace of the world withheld!

ANOTHER WORLD WAR

Stop for a moment to think about the next war! For, I can predict with absolute certainty that within another generation there will be another world war if the nations of the world do not concert the method by which to prevent it. What shall I call it? The final war? It might be the final arrest, though I pray only the temporary arrest, of civilization itself; and America has, if I may take the liberty of saying so, a greater interest in the prevention of that war than any other nation. America is less exhausted by the recent war than the other belligerents; she is not exhausted at all. America has paid for the war that has gone by less heavily, in proportion to her wealth, than the other nations. America still has free capital enough for its own industries and for the industries of the other countries that have to build their industries anew. The next war would have to be paid for in American blood and American money. The nation of all nations that is most interested to prevent the recurrence of what has already happened is the nation which would assuredly have to bear the brunt of that great catastrophe. It is not likely, that with the depleted resources of the great fighting nations of Europe, there will be another war soon, but unless we concert measures to prevent it, there will be another and a final war, just about the time these children come to maturity; and it is our duty to look in the face the real circumstances of the world in order that we may not be unfaithful to the great duty which America undertook in the hour and day of her birth. The next time will come; it will come while this generation is living, and the children will be sacrificed upon the altar of that war. It will be the last war. Humanity will never suffer another, if humanity survives.

I do not hesitate to say that the war we have just been through, though it was shot through with terror of every kind, is not to be compared with the war we would have to face next time. There were destructive gases, there were methods of explosive destruction unheard of even during this war, which were just ready for use when the war ended—great projectiles that guided themselves and shot into the heavens went for a hundred miles and more and then burst tons of explosives upon helpless cities, something to which the guns with which the Germans bombarded Paris from a distance were not comparable. What the Germans used were toys as compared with what would be used in the next war. Ask any soldier if he wants to go through a hell like that again. The soldiers know what the next war would be. They know what the inventions were that were just about to be used for the absolute destruction of mankind. I am for any kind of insurance against a barbaric reversal of civilization.

AMERICA AND MANKIND

Look at the thing in its large aspect, in its majesty. Particularly, look at it as a fulfilment of the destiny of the United States, for it is nothing less. At last, after this long century and more of blood and terror, the world has come to the vision that that little body of 3,000,000 people, strung along the Atlantic coast of this continent had in that far year 1776. Men in Europe laughed at them, at this little handful of dreamers, this little body of men who talked dogmatically about liberty, and since then that fire which they started on that little coast has consumed every autocratic government in the world, every civilized autocratic government, and now at last the flame has leaped to Berlin, and there is the funeral pyre of the German Empire.

America is great because of the ideas she has conceived. America is great because of the purposes she has set herself to achieve. America is not going to be immortal because she has immense wealth. Other nations had immense wealth and went down in decay and disgrace, because they had nothing else. America is great because she has seen visions that other nations have not seen and the one enterprise that does engage the steadfast loyalty and support of the United States is an enterprise for the liberty of mankind. Let gentlemen beware, therefore, how they disappoint the world. Let gentlemen beware, therefore, how they betray the immemorial principles of the United States. Let men not make the mistake of claiming a position of privilege for the United States which gives it all the advantages of the League of Nations and none of the risks and responsibilities. The principle of equity everywhere is that along with a right goes a duty; that if you claim a right for yourself you must be ready to support that right for somebody else; that if you claim to be a member in a society of any sort you must not claim the right to dodge the responsibilities and avoid the burden, but you must carry the weight of the enterprise along with the hope of the enterprise. That is the spirit of free men everywhere, and that I know to be the spirit of the United States.

I will not join in claiming under the name of justice an unjust position of privilege for the country I love and honor. Neither am I afraid of responsibility. Neither will I scuttle. Neither will I be a little American. America, in her make up, in her purposes, in her principles, is the biggest thing in the world, and she must measure up to the measure of the world! I will be no party in belittling her. I will be no party in saying that America is afraid of responsibilities which I know she can carry and in which in carrying I am sure she will lead the world. Why, if we were to decline to go into this humane arrangement we would be declining the invitation which all the world extends to us to lead them in the enterprise of liberty and justice. I, for one, will not decline that invitation. My first thought is how I can help, how I can be effective in the game, how I can make the influence of America tell for the guidance and salvation of the world, not how I can keep out of trouble. I want to get into any kind of trouble that will help liberate mankind!

I, for one, believe more profoundly than in anything else human in the destiny of the United States! I believe that she has a spiritual energy in her which no other nation can

[205]

contribute to the liberation of mankind, and I know that the heart of America is stronger than her business calculations. That is what the world found out when we went into the war. When we went into the war, there was not a nation in the world that did not believe we were more interested in making money out of it than in serving the cause of liberty. And when we went in, in those few months the whole world stood at amaze and ended with an enthusiastic conversion. They now believe that America will stand by anybody that is fighting for justice and for right, and we shall not disappoint them.

I look forward with quickened pulse to the days that lie ahead of us as a member of the League of Nations, for we shall be a member of the League of Nations! I believe in Divine Providence. If I did not, I would go crazy. If I thought the direction of the disordered affairs of this world depended upon our finite intelligence, I should not know how to reason my way to sanity, and I do not believe that there is any body of men, however they concert their power or their influence, that can defeat this great enterprise which is the enterprise of Divine mercy and peace and goodwill.

I look forward with confidence and with exalted hope to the time when we can indeed legitimately and constantly be the champions and friends of those who are struggling for right anywhere in the world. We were respected in those old Revolutionary days when there were three millions of us. We are, it happens, very much more respected now that there are more than a hundred millions of us. Now that we command some of the most important resources of the world, back of the majesty of the United States lies the strength of the United States. No nation is likely to forget that behind the moral judgment of the United States resides the overwhelming force of the United States! So, I look forward with profound gratification to the time when the American people can say to their fellows in all parts of the world, "We are the friends of liberty; we have joined with the rest of mankind in securing the guarantees of liberty; we stand here with you the eternal champions of what is right, and may God keep us in the Covenant that we have formed." God send that day may come, and come soon so that men shall always say that American soldiers saved Europe and American citizens saved the world!

I beg that these things may sink in your thoughts, because we are at a turning point in the fortunes of the world. I beg that you will carry this question with you, not in little pieces, not with this, that and the other detail at the front of your mind, but as a great picture including the whole of the Nation and the whole of Humanity, and know that now is the golden hour when America can at last prove that all she has promised in the day of her birth was no dream but a thing which she saw in its concrete reality, the rights of men, the prosperity of nations, the majesty of justice, and the sacredness of peace.

It is with this solemn thought, that we are at a turning point in the destinies of mankind, and that America is the makeweight of mankind, that I, with perfect confidence, leave this great question to your unbiased judgment.

APPENDICES

A

President Wilson's Address to the Representatives of all the Allied and Associated Nations at the Paris Peace Conference, January 25th, 1919, making it clear beyond all question, the United States had entered the World War with no thought or purpose of intervening in the politics of Europe or of any part of the world, and why a League of Nations was essential for the maintenance of world peace, the matter in which the United States was most concerned. Following this Address, the Paris Peace Conference unanimously agreed that the League of Nations should be an integral part of the Treaty of Versailles.

"I consider it a distinguished privilege to be permitted to open the discussion in this conference on the League of Nations. We have assembled for two purposes: to make the present settlements which have been rendered necessary by this war, and also to secure the peace of the world, not only by the present settlements but by the arrangements we shall make at this conference for its maintenance.

APPENDIX A

The League of Nations seems to me to be necessary for both of these purposes. There are many complicated questions connected with the present settlements which perhaps cannot be successfully worked out to an ultimate issue by the decisions we shall arrive at here. I can easily conceive that many of these settlements will need subsequent consideration, that many of the decisions we make shall need subsequent alteration in some degree; for, if I may judge by my own study of some of these questions, they are not susceptible of confident judgments at present.

"It is, therefore, necessary that we should set up some machinery, by which the work of this conference should be rendered complete. We have assembled here for the purpose of doing very much more than making the present settlements that are necessary. We are assembled under very peculiar conditions of world opinion. I may say without straining the point that we are not representatives of governments, but representatives of peoples. It will not suffice to satisfy governmental circles anywhere. It is necessary that we should satisfy the opinion of mankind. The burdens of this war have fallen in an unusual degree upon the whole population of the countries involved.

"I do not need to draw for you the picture

of how the burden has been thrown back from the front upon the older men, upon the women, upon the children, upon the homes of the civilized world, and how the real strain of the war has come where the eye of the government could not reach, but where the heart of humanity beat. We are bidden by these people to see to it that this strain does not come upon them again, and I venture to say that it has been possible for them to bear this strain because they hoped that those who represented them could get together after this war and make another sacrifice unnecessary.

PLANS FOR PERMANENT PEACE

"It is a solemn obligation on our part, therefore, to make permanent arrangements that justice shall be rendered and peace maintained. This is the central object of our meeting. Settlements may be temporary, but the action of the nations in the interest of peace and justice must be permanent. We can set up permanent processes. We may not be able to set up permanent decisions. Therefore, it seems to me that we must take, so far as we can, a picture of the world into our minds.

"Is it not a startling circumstance, for one thing, that the great discoveries of science, that the quiet studies of men in laboratories, that the thoughtful developments which have taken place in quiet lecture rooms, have now been turned to the destruction of civilization? The powers of destruction have not so much multiplied as gained facility. The enemy whom we have just overcome had at his seats of learning some of the principal centers of scientific study and discovery, and he used them in order to make destruction sudden and complete; and only the watchful, continuous cooperation of men can see to it that science as well as armed men are kept within the harness of civilization.

U. S. CONCERNED FOR WORLD PEACE

"In a sense the United States is less interested in this subject than the other nations here assembled. With her great territory and her extensive sea borders, it is less likely that the United States should suffer from the attack of enemies than that many of the other nations here should suffer; and the ardor of the United States—for it is a very deep and genuine ardor—for the society of nations is not an ardor springing out of fear or apprehension, but an ardor springing out of the ideals which have come to consciousness in this war.

"In coming into this war the United States never for a moment thought that she was intervening in the politics of Europe or the politics of Asia or the politics of any part of the world. Her thought was that all the world had now become conscious that there was a single cause which turned upon the issues of this war. That was the cause of justice and of liberty for men of every kind and place. Therefore the United States should feel that its part in this war had been played in vain if there ensued upon it a body of European settlements. It would feel that it could not take part in guaranteeing those European settlements unless that guarantee involved the continuous superintendence of the peace of the world by the associated nations of the world.

"Therefore, it seems to me that we must concert our best judgment in order to make this League of Nations a vital thing—not merely a formal thing, not an occasional thing, not a thing sometimes called into life to meet an exigency, but always functioning in watchful attendance upon the interests of the nations, and that its continuity should be a vital continuity; that it should have functions that are continuing functions and that do not permit an intermission of its watchfulness and of its labor; that it should be the eye of the nations to keep watch upon the common interest, an eye that did not slumber, an eye that was everywhere watchful and attentive.

"And if we do not make it vital, what shall

we do? We shall disappoint the expectations of the peoples. This is what their thought centers upon. I have had the very delightful experience of visiting several nations since I came to this side of the water, and every time the voice of the body of the people reached me through any representative, at the front of the plea stood the hope for the League of Nations. Gentlemen, the select classes of mankind are no longer the governors of mankind. The fortunes of mankind are now in the hands of the plain people of the whole world. Satisfy them, and you have justified their confidence not only but established peace. Fail to satisfy them, and no arrangement that you can make will either set up or steady the peace of the world.

WHY THE U. S. FAVORED A LEAGUE OF NATIONS

"You can imagine, gentlemen, I dare say, the sentiments and the purposes with which the representatives of the United States support this great project for a League of Nations. We regard it as the keystone of the whole programme, which expressed our purposes and ideals in this war and which the associated nations accepted as the basis of the settlement. If we return to the United States without having made every effort in our power to realize this programme, we should return to meet the merited scorn of our fellow citizens. For they are a body that constitutes a great democracy.

"They expect their leaders to speak their thoughts and no private purpose of their own. They expect their representatives to be their servants. We have no choice but to obey their mandate. But it is with the greatest enthusiasm and pleasure that we accept that mandate; and because this is the keystone of the whole fabric, we have pledged our every purpose to it, as we have to every item of the fabric. We would not dare abate a single item of the program which constitutes our instruction. We would not dare compromise upon any matter as the champion of this thing, this peace of the world, this attitude of justice, this principle that we are the masters of no people but are here to see that every people in the world shall choose its own masters and govern its own destinies, not as we wish but as it wishes.

SWEEP AWAY THE FOUNDATIONS OF THE WAR

"We are here to see, in short, that the very foundations of this war are swept away. Those foundations were the private choice of small coteries of civil rulers and military staffs. Those foundations were the aggression of great powers upon small. Those foundations were the folding together of empires of unwilling subjects by the duress of arms. Those foundations were the power of small bodies of men to work their will and use mankind as pawns in a game. And nothing less than the emancipation of the world from these things will accomplish peace. You can see that the representatives of the United States are, therefore, never put to the embarrassment of choosing a way of expediency, because they have laid down for them the unalterable lines of principle. And, thank God, those lines have been accepted as the lines of settlement by all the high-minded men who have had to do with the beginnings of this great business.

"I hope, Mr. Chairman, that when it is known, as I feel confident it will be known, that we have adopted the principle of the League of Nations and mean to work out that principle in effective action, we shall by that single thing have lifted a great part of the load of anxiety from the hearts of men everywhere. We stand in a peculiar case. As I go about the streets here I see everywhere the American uniform. Those men came into the war after we had uttered our purposes. They came as crusaders, not merely to win a war, but to win a cause; and I am responsible to them, for it fell to me to formulate the purposes for which I asked them to fight, and I, like them, must be a crusader for these things whatever it costs and whatever it may be necessary to do, in honor, to accomplish the object for which they fought.

"I have been glad to find from day to day that there is no question of our standing alone in this matter, for there are champions of this cause upon every hand. I am merely avowing this in order that you may understand why, perhaps, it fell to us, who are disengaged from the politics of this great continent and of the Orient, to suggest that this was the keystone of the arch and why it occurred to the generous mind of our president to call upon me to open this debate. It is not because we alone represent this idea, but because it is our privilege to associate ourselves with you in representing it.

"I have tried in what I have said to give you the fountains of the enthusiasm which is within us for this thing, for those fountains spring, it seems to me, from all the ancient wrongs and sympathies of mankind, and the very pulse of the world seems to beat on the surface in this enterprise."

B

President Wilson's Address giving the Representatives of all the Allied and Associated Powers at the Paris Peace Conference their first official knowledge of the terms in which the Covenant of the League of Nations provides for maintaining the peace of the world and the international cooperation made possible by the common sacrifices of the World War. This Address was followed by the acceptance of the existing Covenant by the Representatives of all the Nations that heard this authoritative explanation.

"Mr. Chairman: I have the honor and as I esteem it the very great privilege of reporting in the name of the Commission constituted by this Conference on the formulation of a plan for the League of Nations. I am happy to say that it is a unanimous report, a unanimous report from the representatives of fourteen nations—the United States, Great Britain, France, Italy, Japan, Belgium, Brazil, China, Czecho-Slovakia, Greece, Poland, Portugal, Roumania and Serbia. I think it will be serviceable and interesting if I, with your permission, read the document as the only report we have to make."

President Wilson then proceeded to read the Covenant. When he reached Article XV and had read through the second paragraph, he paused and said:

"I pause to point out that a misconception might arise in connection with one of the sentences I have just read. "If any party shall refuse to comply, the council shall propose measures necessary to give effect to the recommendations.

"A case in point, a purely hypothetical case, is this: Suppose there is in the possession of a particular power a piece of territory or some other substantial thing in dispute, to which it is claimed that it is not entitled. Suppose that the matter is submitted to the Executive Council for recommendation as to the settlement of the dispute, diplomacy having failed, and suppose that the decision is in favor of the party which claims the subject matter of dispute, as against the party which has the subject matter in dispute. Then, if the party in possession of the subject matter in dispute merely sits still and does nothing, it has accepted the decision of the Council in the sense that it makes no resistance, but something must be done to see that it surrenders the subject matter in dispute.

"In such a case, the only case contemplated, it is provided that the Executive Council may then consider what steps may be necessary to oblige the party against whom judgment has been given to comply with the decisions of the Council."

After reading Article XIX, President Wilson also stopped and said:

"Let me say that before being embodied in this document this was the subject matter of very careful discussion by representatives of the five greater parties and that their unanimous conclusion is the matter embodied in this Article."

After reading the Covenant throughout, President Wilson proceeded:

"It gives me pleasure to add to this formal reading of the result of our labors that the character of the discussion which occurred at the sittings of the Commission was not only of the most constructive but of the most encouraging sort. It was obvious throughout our discussions that, although there were subjects upon which there were individual differences of judgment, with regard to the method by which our objects should be obtained, there was practically at no point any serious difference of opinion as to the objects which we were seeking. Indeed, while these debates were not made the opportunity for the expression of enthusiasms and sentiments, I think the other members of the Commission will agree with me that there was an undertone of high respect and of enthusiasm for the thing we were trying to do, which was heartening throughout every meeting, because we felt that in a way this Conference had entrusted to us the expression of one of its highest and most important purposes, to see to it that the concord of the world in the future with regard to the objects of justice should not be subject to doubt or uncertainty, that the cooperation of the great body of nations should be assured from the first in the maintenance of peace upon the terms of honor and of strict regard for international obligation. The compulsion of that task was constantly upon us, and at no point was there shown the slightest desire to do anything but suggest the best means to accomplish that great object. There is very great significance, therefore, in the fact that the result was reached unanimously.

"Fourteen nations were represented, among them all of those powers which for convenience we have called the Great Powers, and among the rest a representation of the greatest variety of circumstance and interest. So I think we are justified in saying that it was a representative group of the members of this great conference. The significance of the result, therefore, has that deepest of all meanings, the union of wills in a common purpose, a union of wills which cannot be resisted, and which I dare say no nation will run the risk of attempting to resist.

THE LEAGUE SIMPLE

"Now as to the character of the result. While it has consumed some time to read this document, I think you will see at once that it is, after all, very simple, and in nothing so simple as in the structure which it suggests for the League of Nations—a body of Delegates, an Executive Council, and a Permanent Secretariat. When it came to the question of determining the character of the representation in the body of delegates, we were all aware of a feeling which is current throughout the world. Inasmuch as I am stating it in the presence of official representatives of the various Governments here present, including myself, I may say that there is a universal feeling that the world cannot rest satisfied with merely official guidance.

"There has reached us through many channels the feeling that if the deliberative body of the League of Nations was merely to be a body of officials representing the various governments, the peoples of the world would not be sure that some of the mistakes which pre-occupied officials had admittedly made might not be repeated. It was impossible to conceive a method or an assembly so large and various as to be really representative of the great body of the peoples of the world, because, as I roughly reckon it, we represent as we sit around this table more than twelve hundred million people.

"You cannot have a representative assembly of twelve hundred million people, but if you leave it to each government to have, if it pleases, one or two or three representatives, though only a single vote, it may vary its representation from time to time, not only, but it may govern the choice of its several representatives, if it should have several, in different ways.

VARIETY OF REPRESENTATION

"Therefore, we thought that this was a proper and a very prudent concession to the practically universal opinion of plain men everywhere that they wanted the door left open to a variety of representation instead of being confined to a single official body with which they might or might not find themselves in sympathy.

"And you will notice that this body has unlimited rights of discussion—I mean of discussion of anything that falls within the field of international relationship—and that it is especially agreed that war or international misunderstandings or anything that may lead to friction and trouble is everybody's business, because it may affect the peace of the world. And in order to safeguard the popular power so far as we could of this representative body, it is provided you will notice, that when a subject is submitted, not to arbitration, but to discussion by the executive council, it can, be drawn out of the executive council to the larger forum of the general body of the delegates, because throughout this instrument we are depending primarily and chiefly upon one great force, and that is the moral force of the public opinion of the world—the pleasing and clarifying and compelling influences of publicity; so that intrigues can no longer have their coverts, so that designs that are sinister can at any time be drawn into the open, so that those things that are destroyed by the light may be promptly destroyed by the overwhelming light of the universal expression of the condemnation of the world.

"Armed force is in the background in this program, but it *is* in the background, and if the moral force of the world will not suffice, the physical force of the world shall. But that is the last resort, because this is intended as a constitution of peace, not as a league of war.

NOT A STRAITJACKET

"The simplicity of the document seems to me to be one of its chief virtues, because, speaking for myself, I was unable to foresee the variety of circumstances with which this League would have to deal. I was unable, therefore, to plan all the machinery that might be necessary to meet differing and unexpected contingencies. Therefore, I should say of this document that it is not a strait jacket but a vehicle of life. A living thing is born, and we must see to it that the clothes we put upon it do not hamper it. It is a vehicle of power, but a vehicle in which power may be varied at the discretion of those who exercise it and in accordance with the changing circumstances of the time. And yet, while it is elastic, while it is general in its terms, it is definite in the one thing that we are called upon to make definite: It is a definite guarantee of peace. It is a definite guarantee against aggression. It is a definite guarantee against the things which have just come near bringing the whole structure of civilization to the brink of ruin.

APPENDIX B

LABOR GIVEN NEW STATUS

"Its purposes do not for a moment lie vague. Its purposes are declared, and its powers made unmistakable. It is not in contemplation that this should be merely a League to secure the peace of the world. It is a League which can be used for cooperation in any international matter. That is the significance of the provision introduced concerning labor. There are many ameliorations of labor conditions which can be effected by conference and discussion. I anticipate that there will be a very great usefulness in the bureau of labor which it is contemplated shall be set up by the League. While men and women who work have been in the background through long ages, and sometimes seem to be forgotten, while governments have had their watchful and suspicious eyes upon the maneuvers of one another, while the thought of statesmen has been about structural action and the large transactions of commerce and of finance.

"Now, if I may believe the picture which I see, there comes into the foreground the great body of the laboring people of the world, the men and women and children upon whom the great burden of sustaining the world must from day to day fall, whether we wish it to do so or not; people who go to bed tired and wake up without the stimulation of lively hope. These people will be drawn into the field of international consultation and help, and will be among the wards of the combined governments of the world. There is, I take leave to say, a very great step in advance in the mere conception of that.

TREATIES MUST BE PUBLISHED

"Then, as you will notice, there is an imperative article concerning the publicity of all international agreements. Henceforth no member of the League can claim any agreement valid which it has not registered with the Secretary General, in whose office, of course, it will be subject to the examination of anybody representing a member of the League. And the duty is laid upon the Secretary General to publish every document of that sort at the earliest possible time.

"I suppose most persons who have not been conversant with the business of foreign offices do not realize how many hundreds of these agreements are made in a single year, and how difficult it might be to publish the more unimportant of them immediately—how uninteresting it would be to most of the world to publish them immediately, but even they must be published just as soon as it is possible for the Secretary General to publish them.

"Then there is a feature about this Covenant which to my mind is one of the greatest and most satisfactory advances that have been made. We are done with annexations of helpless people, meant in some instances by some powers to be used merely for exploitation. We recognized in the most solemn manner that the helpless and undeveloped peoples of the world, being in that condition, put an obligation upon us to look after their interests primarily before we use them for our interests; and that in all cases of this sort hereafter it shall be the duty of the League to see that the nations who are assigned as the tutors and advisers and directors of those people shall look to their interest and to their development before they look to the interests and material desires of the mandatory nation itself.

"There has been no greater advance than this, gentlemen. If you look back upon the history of the world you will see how helpless peoples have too often been a prey to powers that had no conscience in the matter. It has been one of the many distressing revelations of recent years that the Great Power which has just been, happily, defeated put intolerable burdens and injustices upon the helpless people of some of the colonies which it annexed to itself; that its interest was rather their extermination than their development;

that the desire was to possess their land for European purposes, and not to enjoy their confidence in order that mankind might be lifted in those places to the next higher level.

"Now, the world, expressing its conscience in law, says there is an end of that, that our consciences shall be applied to this thing. States will be picked out which have already shown that they can exercise a conscience in this matter, and under their tutelage the helpless peoples of the world will come into a new light and into a new hope.

SYMPATHY IN IT

"So I think I can say of this document that it is at one and the same time a practical document and a humane document. There is a pulse of sympathy in it. There is a compulsion of conscience throughout it. It is practical, and yet it is intended to purify, to rectify, to elevate. And I want to say that, so far as my observation instructs me, this is in one sense a belated document. I believe that the conscience of the world has long been prepared to express itself in some such way. We are not just now discovering our sympathy for these people and our interest in them. We are simply expressing it, for it has long been felt, and in the administration of the affairs of more than one of the great States represented here

—so far as I know, of all the great States that are represented here—that humane impulse has already expressed itself in their dealings with their colonies, whose peoples were yet at a low stage of civilization.

"We have had many instances of colonies lifted into the sphere of complete self-government. This is not the discovery of a principle. It is the universal application of a principle. It is the agreement of the great nations which have tried to live by these standards in their separate administrations to unite in seeing that their common force and their common thought and intelligence are lent to this great and humane enterprise. I think it is an occasion, therefore, for the most profound satisfaction that this humane decision should have been reached in a matter for which the world has long been waiting and until a very recent period thought that it was still too early to hope.

"Many terrible things have come out of this war, gentlemen, but some very beautiful things have come out of it. Wrong has been defeated, but the rest of the world has been more conscious than it ever was before of the majesty of right. People that were suspicious of one another can now live as friends and comrades in a single family, and desire to do so. The miasma of distrust, of intrigue, is cleared away. Men are looking eye to eye and saying, 'We are brothers and have a common purpose. We did not realize it before, but now we do realize it, and this is our Covenant of fraternity and of friendship'."

C

President Wilson's Advisers, the American Experts—at the Paris Peace Conference.

The Official Commissioners representing the United States at the Conference, were President Wilson, Hon. Robert Lansing, Secretary of State, Hon. Henry White, formerly United States Ambassador at Paris and at Rome, Hon. Edward M. House and General Tasker H. Bliss, United States Army.

To the courtesy of Mr. George Creel and Mr. Thomas W. Lamont, I am indebted for permission to quote two of the many interesting official and public statements made by President Wilson as to his entire confidence in and dependence upon the gentlemen whose names appear in this Appendix, during the important work of the Peace Conference.

Mr. Creel has made of record in his book, "The War, The World, and Wilson," how President Wilson, on the way to Paris, assured these gentlemen:

"You are, in truth, my advisers, for when I ask you for information I will have no way of checking it up, and must act upon it unquestioningly. We will be deluged with claims plausibly and convincingly presented. It will be your task to establish the truth or falsity of these claims out of your specialized knowledge, so that my positions may be taken fairly and intelligently."

Mr. Lamont has testified:

"I never saw a man more considerate of those of his coadjutors who were working immediately with him, nor a man more ready to give them credit with the other chiefs of state. Again and again he would say to Mr. Lloyd George or Mr. Clemenceau: "My expert here, Mr. So-and-So, tells me such and such, and I believe he is right. You will have to argue with him if you want me to change my opinion."

Economic and Commercial Questions

BERNARD M. BARUCH	ALEX. LEGG
VANCE MCCORMICK	CHARLES MCDOWELL
FRANK W. TAUSSIG	LELAND SUMMERS

Financial Questions

NORMAN H. DAVIS	THOMAS W. LAMONT
JOHN FOSTER DULLES	ALBERT STRAUSS

Judicial Questions

DAVID HUNTER MILLER	JAMES C. PENNIE
JAMES BROWN SCOTT	FREDERICK NEILSON
CHANDLER ANDERSON	

Questions of Ways and Means

HERBERT HOOVER

APPENDIX C

Questions of Navigation and Labor

E. N. HURLEY   SAMUEL GOMPERS

Questions of Naval Affairs

Admiral W. S. BENSON, U. S. Navy

Questions of Military Affairs

Major General F. J. KERNAN, U. S. Army

Technical Experts

Doctor SIDNEY E. MEZES, Director

*Chief Territorial Adviser and Executive Officer of the Section
of Territorial, Economic and Political Intelligence*

Doctor ISAIAH BOWMAN

Questions of Economics and Statistics

Professor ALLYN A. YOUNG

Questions of Ethnography

Professor ROLAND B. DIXON   Captain W. C. FARABEE

Questions of History

Professor JAMES T. SHOTWELL

Questions of Geography

Professor MARK JEFFERSON

Questions as to Colonies

GEORGE LOUIS BEER

Questions as to Germany

Doctor WALLACE NOTESTEIN

Questions as to Austria-Hungary

Professor CHARLES SEYMOUR

Questions as to Turkey

Professor W. L. WESTERMANN

Questions as to the Balkans

Professor CLIVE DAY

APPENDIX C

Questions as to Alsace-Lorraine and Belgium

Professor CHARLES H. HASKINS

Questions as to the Orient

Captain S. K. HORNBECK   Professor E. T. WILLIAMS

Questions as to Italy

Professor W. E. LUNT   Major D. W. JOHNSON

Questions as to Russia and Poland

Professor R. H. LORD   Doctor ISAIAH BOWMAN

Secretary General

Hon. JOSEPH CLARK GREW, Minister Plenipotentiary

Secretaries

ARTHUR HUGH FRAZIER	LELAND HARRISON
Colonel U. S. GRANT, 3rd.	ALEXANDER C. KIRK
CHRISTIAN A. HERTER	PHILIP H. PATCHIN
GRAFTON WINTHROP MINOT	GORDON AUCHINCLOSS
Lt. CHESTER BURDEN, U.S.A.	Capt. JAMES A. GARFIELD

Capt. VAN S. MERLE-SMITH, U.S.A.

Political and Diplomatic Advisers

ELLIS LORING DRESEL, Chief of Section

JORDAN HERBERT STABLER, Chief of the Latin American Bureau of the Department of State

FREDERIC R. DOLBEARE	ALLEN W. DULLES
E. T. WILLIAMS	SIDNEY Y. SMITH

J. F. D. PAUL, Attache

D

*Some Facts Not Generally Known to Students
and to Critics of the Covenant of the League
of Nations.*

The following copies of official cablegrams
show how President Wilson, when at the Paris
Peace Conference, received and welcomed the
suggestions as to changes in the Covenant of
the League of Nations proposed by former
President William H. Taft and former Secretary of State, Elihu Root.

The Covenant referred to in these cable-
grams was the first form of that document
President Wilson had brought from Paris and
discussed with the Members of the Foreign
Relations Committee of the Senate and the
Foreign Affairs Committee of the House of
Representatives.

When it is remembered that Mr. Root because of his record as one of the foremost international lawyers of the world, was specially
invited by many of the distinguished jurists
of Europe to be one of the men to establish
the existing World Court; and that Mr. Taft
is now the Chief Justice of the United States

Supreme Court, the thoughtful reader and student of the League will find it interesting to note what modifications such eminent American lawyers believed would make the Covenant entirely acceptable to the United States Senate. A comparison of the suggestions made by Mr. Taft and Mr. Root, with the Covenant as it is today, will prove that before it was adopted in its final form by all the Nations represented at the Paris Peace Conference, and before he submitted it to the United States Senate, President Wilson succeeded in having written into it practically every suggestion made by Mr. Taft and by Mr. Root, either in the language they proposed or in terms that very specifically provide for the matters they wished made definite.   H. F.

Cablegram

The White House, Washington,
16 March, 1919

PRESIDENT WILSON,
Paris.

Former President Taft asks if he may cable to you direct, for your consideration only, some suggestions about which he has been thinking a great deal and which he would like to have you consider. He said that these suggestions do not look to the change of the structure of the League, the plan of its action or its real character, but simply to removing objections in minds of conscientious Americans, who are anxious for a league of nations, whose fears have been aroused by

APPENDIX D

suggested constructions of the League which its language does not justify and whose fears could be removed without any considerable change of language.

TUMULTY.

Cablegram-Paris

Received at White House
March 18, 1919

In reply to your number sixteen, appreciate Mr. Taft's offer suggestions and would welcome them. The sooner they are sent the better. You need give yourself no concern about my yielding anything with regard to the embodiment of the proposed convention with Turkey.

WOODROW WILSON.

Cablegram.

The White House, Washington.
18 March, 1919

PRESIDENT WILSON
Paris.

Following from Wm. H. Taft.

"If you bring back the Treaty with the League of Nations in it, make more specific reservations of the Monroe Doctrine, fix a term for the duration of the League and the limit of armament, require expressly unanimity of action in Executive Council and body of Delegates, and add to Article XV a provision that where the Executive Council of the Body of Delegates finds the difference to grow out of an exclusively domestic policy, it shall recommend no settlement, the ground will be completely cut from under the opponents of the League in the Senate. Addition to Article XV will answer objection as to Japanese immigration as well as tariffs under Article XXI. Reservation of the Monroe Doctrine might be as follows:

[240]

APPENDIX D

Any American state or states may protect the integrity of American territory and the independence of the government whose territory it is, whether a member of the League or not, and may, in the interests of American peace, object to and prevent the further transfer of American territory or sovereignty to any European or non-American power.

Monroe Doctrine reservation alone would probably carry the treaty but the others would make it certain. (Signed Wm. H. Taft.)"   TUMULTY.

Cablegram

The White House, Washington.
21 March, 1919.

PRESIDENT WILSON,
Paris.

The following letter from Hon. Wm. H. Taft.

"I have thought perhaps it might help more if I was somewhat more specific than I was in the memorandum note I sent you yesterday, and I therefore enclose another memorandum.

DURATION OF THE COVENANT

Add to the Preamble the following:

"From the obligations of which any member of the League may withdraw after July 1, 1929, by two years notice in writing, duly filed with the Secretary General of the League."

Explanation

I have no doubt that the construction put upon the agreement would be what I understand the President has already said it should be, namely that any nation may withdraw from it upon reasonable notice, which perhaps would be a year. I think, however, it might strengthen the Covenant if there was a fixed duration. It would completely remove the objection that it is perpetual in its operation.

DURATION OF ARMAMENT LIMIT

Add to the first paragraph of Article VIII, the following:

"At the end of every five years, such limits of armament for the several governments shall be re-examined by the Executive Council, and agreed upon by them as in the first instance."

Explanation

The duration of the obligation to limit armament, which now may only be changed by consent of the Executive Council, has come in for criticism. I should think this might be avoided, without in any way injuring the Covenant. Perhaps three years is enough, but I should think five years would be better.

Unanimous Action by the Executive Council or Body of Delegates

Insert in Article IV, after the first paragraph, the following:

"Other action taken or recommendations made by the Executive Council or body of Delegates shall be by the unanimous action of the countries represented by the members or delegates, unless otherwise specifically stated."

Explanation

Great objection is made to the power of the Executive Council by a majority of the members and the Body of Delegates to do the things which they are authorized to do in the Covenant. In view of the specific provision that the Executive Council and the Body of Delegates may act by a majority of its members as to their procedure, I feel confident that, except in cases where otherwise provided, both bodies can only act by unanimous vote of the countries represented. If that be the right construction, then there can be no objection to have it specifically stated, and it will remove emphatic objection already made on this ground. It is a complete safeguard against involving the United States primarily in small distant wars to which the United States has no immediate relation, for the reason that the plan for taking care of such a war, to be recommended or advised by the Executive Council, must be approved by a representative of the United States on the Board.

MONROE DOCTRINE

Add to Article X

(a) "A state or states of America, a member or members of the League, and competent to fulfill this obligation in respect to American territory or independence, may, in event of the aggression, actual or threatened, expressly assume the obligation and relieve the European or non-American members of the League from it until they shall be advised by such American state or states of the need for their aid."

(b) "Any such American state or states may protect the integrity of any American territory and the sovereignty of the government whose territory it is, whether a member of the League or not, and may, in the interest of American peace, object to and prevent the further transfer of American territory or sovereignty to any American or non-American power."

APPENDIX D

Explanation

Objection has been made that under Article X, European governments would come to America with force and be concerned in matters from which heretofore the United States has excluded them. This is not true, because Spain fought Chili, in Seward's time, without objection from the United States, and so Germany and England instituted a blockade against Venezuela in Roosevelt's time. This fear could be removed, however, by the first of the above paragraphs.

Paragraph (*b*) is the Monroe Doctrine pure and simple. I forwarded this in my first memorandum. It will be observed that Article X only covers the integrity and independence of members of the League. There may be some American countries which are not sufficiently responsible to make it wise to invite them into the League. This second paragraph covers them. The expression "European or non-American" is inserted for the purpose of indicating that Great Britain, though it has American dominion, is not to acquire further territority or sovereignty.

JAPANESE IMMIGRATION AND TARIFFS

Add to Article XV

"If the difference between the parties shall be found by the Executive Council or the Body of Delegates to be a question which by international law is solely within the domestic jurisdiction and polity of one of the parties, it shall so report and not recommend a settlement of the dispute."

Explanation

Objection is made to Article XV that under its terms the United States would be bound by unanimous recommendation for settlement of a dispute in respect to any issue foreign or domestic; that it therefore might be affected seriously, and unjustly, by recommendation forbidding tariffs on importations. In my judgment, we could only rely on the public opinion of the world evidenced by the Body of Delegates, not to interfere with our domestic legislation and action. Nor do I think that under the League as it is, we covenant to abide by a unanimous recommendation. But if there is a specific exception made in respect to matters completely within the domestic jurisdiction and legislation of a country, the whole criticism is removed. The Republican senators are trying to stir up anxiety among Republicans lest this be a limitation upon our tariff. The President has already specifically met the objection as to limitation upon the tariff when the Fourteen points were under discussion. Nevertheless in this respect to the present language of the Covenant, it would help much to meet and remove objections, and cut the ground under senatorial obstructions.

PROSPECT OF RATIFICATION

My impression is that if the one article already sent, on the Monroe Doctrine, be inserted in the Treaty, sufficient Republicans who signed the Round Robin would probably retreat from their position and vote for ratification so that it would carry. If the other suggestions were adopted, I feel confident that all but a few who oppose any league would be driven to accept them and to stand for the League."

(End Letter)   TUMULTY.

APPENDIX D

Admission—Paris.

For Secretary Lansing from Polk.

Following are proposed amendments to the Constitution of the League of Nations which have been drafted by Mr. Root.

First Amendment: Strike out Article XIII, and insert the following:

> The high contracting powers agree to refer to the existing Permanent Court of Arbitration at the Hague, or to the Court of Arbitral Justice proposed at the Second Hague Conference when established, or to some other tribunal, all disputes between them (including those affecting honour and vital interests) which are of a justiciable character, and which the powers concerned have failed to settle by diplomatic methods. The powers so referring to arbitration agree to accept and give effect to the award of the Tribunal.
>
> Disputes of a justiciable character are defined as disputes as to the interpretation of a treaty, as to any question of international law, as to the existence of any fact which if established would constitute a breach of any international obligation, or as to the nature and extent of the reparation to be made for any such breach.
>
> Any question which may arise as to whether a dispute is of a justiciable character is to be referred for decision to the Court of Arbitral Justice when constituted, or, until it is constituted, to the existing Permanent Court of Arbitration at the Hague.

Second Amendment. Add to Article XIV the following paragraphs:

> The Executive Council shall call a general conference of the powers to meet not less than two years

or more than five years after the signing of this convention for the purpose of reviewing the condition of international law, and of agreeing upon and stating in authoritative form the principles and rules thereof.

Thereafter, regular conferences for that purpose shall be called and held at stated intervals.

Third Amendment. Immediately before the signature of the American Delegates, insert the following reservation:

Inasmuch as in becoming a member of the League the United States of America is moved by no interest or wish to intrude upon or interfere with the political policy or internal administration of any foreign state, and by no existing or anticipated dangers in the affairs of the American continents, but accedes to the wish of the European states that it shall join its power to theirs for the preservation of general peace, the representatives of the United States of America sign this convention with the understanding that nothing therein contained shall be construed to imply a relinquishment by the United States of America of its traditional attitude towards purely American questions, or to require the submission of its policy regarding such questions (including therein the admission of immigrants) to the decision or recommendation of other powers.

Fourth Amendment. Add to Article X the following: After the expiration of five years from the beginning of this convention any party may terminate its obligations under this article by giving one year's notice in writing to the Secretary General of the League.

Fifth Amendment. Add to Article IX the following: Such commission shall have full power of inspection and verification personally and by authorized agents as to all armament, equipment, munitions and industries referred to in Article VIII.

Sixth Amendment. Add to Article XXIV the following: The Executive Council shall call a general conference of members of the League to meet not less than five nor more than ten years after the signing of this convention for the revision thereof, and at that time, or any time thereafter upon one year's notice, any member may withdraw from the League.

POLK, *Acting.*

E

The Assembly on Sept. 27, 1922, expressed the opinion "the obligation to render assistance to a country attacked shall be limited in principle to those countries situated in the same part of the globe." This confirms absolutely Mr. Wilson's sentences.

When this book went to press the Assembly of the League had before it the report of its Disarmament Commission. Article Eleven of that reads: "No high contracting parties shall be under obligation in principle to co-operate in a continent, other than the one in which they are situated, in military, naval or air operation undertaken in connection with the general or supplementary assistance provided for by this Treaty." H.F.

F

THE COVENANT OF THE LEAGUE OF NATIONS

THE HIGH CONTRACTING PARTIES

In order to promote international cooperation
and to achieve international peace and security
by the acceptance of obligations not to resort
to war,
by the prescription of open, just and honourable relations between nations,
by the firm establishment of the understandings of international law as the actual rule of
conduct among Governments, and
by the maintenance of justice and a scrupulous
respect for all treaty obligations in the dealings
of organized peoples with one another,
Agree to this Covenant of the League of Nations.

ARTICLE I

The original Members of the League of Nations
shall be those of the Signatories which are named
in the Annex to this Covenant and also such of
those other States named in the Annex as shall
accede without reservation to this Covenant.
Such accession shall be effected by a Declaration
deposited with the Secretariat within two months

of the coming into force of the Covenant. Notice thereof shall be sent to all other Members of the League.

Any fully self-governing State, Dominion, or Colony not named in the Annex may become a Member of the League if its admission is agreed to by two-thirds of the Assembly, provided that it shall give effective guarantees of its sincere intention to observe its international obligations, and shall accept such regulations as may be prescribed by the League in regard to its military, naval, and air forces and armaments.

Any Member of the League may, after two years' notice of its intention so to do, withdraw from the League, provided that all its international obligations and all its obligations under this Covenant shall have been fulfilled at the time of its withdrawal.

ARTICLE 2

The action of the League under this Covenant shall be effected through the instrumentality of an Assembly and of a Council, with a permanent Secretariat,

ARTICLE 3

The Assembly shall consist of Representatives of the Members of the League.

The Assembly shall meet at stated intervals and from time to time as occasion may require at the Seat of the League or at such other place as may be decided upon.

APPENDIX F

The Assembly may deal at its meetings with any matter within the sphere of action of the League or affecting the peace of the world.

At meetings of the Assembly each Member of the League shall have one vote, and may not have more than three Representatives.

The Council shall consist of Representatives of the Principal Allied and Associated Powers, together with Representatives of four other Members of the League. These four Members of the League shall be selected by the Assembly from time to time in its discretion. Until the appointment of the Representatives of the four Members of the League first selected by the Assembly, Representatives of Belgium, Brazil, Spain, and Greece shall be members of the Council.

With the approval of the majority of the Assembly, the Council may name additional Members of the League whose Representatives shall always be members of the Council; the Council with like approval may increase the number of Members of the League to be selected by the Assembly for representation on the Council.

The Council shall meet from time to time as occasion may require, and at least once a year, at the Seat of the League, or at such other place as may be decided upon.

The Council may deal at its meetings with any

matter within the sphere of action of the League or affecting the peace of the world.

Any Member of the League not represented on the Council shall be invited to send a Representative to sit as a member at any meeting of the Council during the consideration of matters specially affecting the interests of that Member of the League.

At meetings of the Council, each Member of the League represented on the Council shall have one vote, and may have not more than one Representative.

ARTICLE 5

Except where otherwise expressly provided in this Covenant or by the terms of the present Treaty, decisions at any meeting of the Assembly or of the Council shall require the agreement of all the Members of the League represented by the meeting.

All matters of procedure at meetings of the Assembly or of the Council, including the appointment of Committees to investigate particular matters, shall be regulated by the Assembly or by the Council and may be decided by a majority of the Members of the League represented at the meeting.

The first meeting of the Assembly and the first meeting of the Council shall be summoned by the President of the United States of America.

APPENDIX F

The permanent Secretariat shall be established at the Seat of the League. The Secretariat shall comprise a Secretary General and such secretaries and staff as may be required.

The first Secretary General shall be the person named in the Annex; thereafter the Secretary General shall be appointed by the Council with the approved of the majority of the Assembly.

The secretaries and staff of the Secretariat shall be appointed by the Secretary General with the approval of the Council.

The Secretary General shall act in that capacity at all meetings of the Assembly and of the Council.

The expenses of the Secretariat shall be borne by the Members of the League in accordance with the apportionment of the expenses of the International Bureau of the Universal Postal Union.

ARTICLE 7

The Seat of the League is established at Geneva.

The Council may at any time decide that the Seat of the League shall be established elsewhere.

All positions under or in connection with the League, including the Secretariat, shall be open equally to men and women.

Representatives of the Members of the League and officials of the League when engaged on the business of the League shall enjoy diplomatic privileges and immunities.

APPENDIX F

The buildings and other property occupied by the League or its officials or by Representatives attending its meetings shall be inviolable.

ARTICLE 8

The Members of the League recognize that the maintenance of peace requires the reduction of national armaments to the lowest point consistent with national safety and the enforcement by common action of international obligations.

The Council, taking account of the geographical situation and circumstances of each State, shall formulate plans for such reduction for the consideration and action of the several Governments.

Such plans shall be subject to reconsideration and revision at least every ten years.

After these plans shall have been adopted by the several Governments, the limits of armaments therein fixed shall not be exceeded without the concurrence of the Council.

The Members of the League agree that the manufacture by private enterprise of munitions and implements of war is open to grave objections. The Council shall advise how the evil effects attendant upon such manufacture can be prevented, due regard being had to the necessities of those Members of the League which are not able to manufacture the munitions and implements of war necessary for their safety.

APPENDIX F

The Members of the League undertake to interchange full and frank information as to the scale of their armaments, their military, naval, and air programmes and the condition of such of their industries as are adaptable to war-like purposes.

ARTICLE 9

A permanent Commission shall be constituted to advise the Council on the execution of the provisions of Articles 1 and 8 and on military, naval, and air questions generally.

ARTICLE 10

The Members of the League undertake to respect and preserve as against external aggression the territorial integrity and existing political independence of all Members of the League. In case of any such aggression or in case of any threat or danger of such aggression the Council shall advise upon the means by which this obligation shall be fulfilled.

ARTICLE 11

Any war or threat of war, whether immediately affecting any of the Members of the League or not, is hereby declared a matter of concern to the whole League, and the League shall take any action that may be deemed wise and effectual to safeguard the peace of nations. In case any such emergency should arise the Secretary General shall on the request of any Member of the League forthwith summon a meeting of the Council.

It is also declared to be the friendly right of each Member of the League to bring to the attention of the Assembly or of the Council any circumstance whatever affecting international relations which threatens to disturb international peace or the good understanding between nations upon which peace depends.

ARTICLE 12

The Members of the League agree that if there should arise between them any dispute likely to lead to a rupture, they will submit the matter either to arbitration or to inquiry by the Council, and they agree in no case to resort to war until three months after the award by the arbitrators or the report by the Council.

In any case under this Article the award of the arbitrators shall be made within a reasonable time, and the report of the Council shall be made within six months after the submission of the dispute.

ARTICLE 13

The Members of the League agree that whenever any dispute shall arise between them which they recognize to be suitable for submission to arbitration and which cannot be satisfactorily settled by diplomacy, they will submit the whole subject-matter to arbitration.

APPENDIX F

Disputes as to the interpretation of a treaty, as to any question of international law, as to the existence of any fact which if established would constitute a breach of any international obligation, or as to the extent and nature of the reparation to be made for any such breach, are declared to be among those which are generally suitable for submission to arbitration.

For the consideration of any such dispute the court of arbitration to which the case is referred shall be the Court agreed on by the parties to the dispute or stipulated in any convention existing between them.

The Members of the League agree that they will carry out in full good faith any award that may be rendered, and that they will not resort to war against a Member of the League which complies therewith. In the event of any failure to carry out such an award, the Council shall propose what steps should be taken to give effect thereto.

ARTICLE 14

The Council shall formulate and submit to the Members of the League for adoption plans for the establishment of a Permanent Court of International Justice. The Court shall be competent to hear and determine any dispute of an international character which the parties thereto submit to it. The Court may also give an advisory opinion upon any dispute or question referred to it by the Council or by the Assembly.

ARTICLE 15

If there should arise between Members of the League any dispute likely to lead to a rupture, which is not submitted to arbitration in accordance with Article 13, the Members of the League agree that they will submit the matter to the Council. Any party to the dispute may effect such submission by giving notice of the existence of the dispute to the Secretary General, who will make all necessary arrangements for a full investigation and consideration thereof.

For this purpose the parties to the dispute will communicate to the Secretary General, as promptly as possible, statements of their case with all the relevant facts and papers, and the Council may forthwith direct the publication thereof.

The Council shall endeavor to effect a settlement of the dispute, and if such efforts are successful, a statement shall be made public giving such facts and explanations regarding the dispute and the terms of settlement thereof as the Council may deem appropriate.

If the dispute is not thus settled, the Council either unanimously or by a majority vote shall make and publish a report containing a statement of the facts of the dispute and the recommendations which are deemed just and proper in regard thereto.

Any Member of the League represented on the Council may make public a statement of the facts of the dispute and of its conclusions regarding the same.

If a report by the Council is unanimously agreed to by the members thereof other than the Representatives of one or more of the parties to the dispute, the Members of the League agree that they will not go to war with any party to the dispute which complies with the recommendations of the report.

If the Council fails to reach a report which is unanimously agreed to by the members thereof, other than the Representatives of one or more of the parties to the dispute, the Members of the League reserve to themselves the right to take such action as they shall consider necessary for the maintenance of right and justice.

If the dispute between the parties is claimed by one of them, and is found by the Council, to arise out of a matter which by international law is solely within the domestic jurisdiction of that party, the Council shall so report, and shall make no recommendation as to its settlement.

The Council may in any case under this Article refer the dispute to the Assembly. The dispute shall be so referred at the request of either party to the dispute, provided that such request be made within fourteen days after the submission of the dispute to the Council.

In any case referred to the Assembly, all the provisions of this Article and of Article 12 relating to the action and powers of the Council shall apply to the action and powers of the Assembly, provided that a report made by the Assembly, if concurred in by the Representatives of those Members of the League represented on the Council and of a majority of the other Members of the League, exclusive in each case of the Representatives of the parties to the dispute, shall have the same force as a report by the Council concurred in by all the members thereof other than the Representatives of one or more of the parties to the dispute.

ARTICLE 16

Should any Member of the League resort to war in disregard of its covenants under Articles 12, 13, or 15, it shall *ipso facto* be deemed to have committed an act of war against all other Members of the League, which hereby undertake immediately to subject it to the severance of all trade or financial relations, the prohibition of all intercourse between their nationals and the nationals of the covenant-breaking State, and the prevention of all financial, commercial, or personal intercourse between the nationals of the covenant-breaking State and the nationals of any other State, whether a Member of the League or not.

It shall be the duty of the Council in such case to recommend to the several Governments concerned what effective military, naval, or air force the Members of the League shall severally contribute to the armed forces to be used to protect the covenants of the League.

The Members of the League agree, further, that they will mutually support one another in the financial and economic measures which are taken under this Article, in order to minimize the loss and inconvenience resulting from the above measures, and that they will mutually support one another in resisting any special measures aimed at one of their number by the covenant, breaking State, and that they will take the necessary steps to afford passage through their territory to the forces of any of the Members of the League which are cooperating to protect the covenants of the League.

Any Member of the League which has violated any covenant of the League may be declared to be no longer a Member of the League by a vote of the Council concurred in by the Representatives of all the other Members of the League represented thereon.

ARTICLE 17

In the event of a dispute between a Member of the League and a State which is not a Member of the League, or between States not Members of the League, the State or States, not Members of the League shall be invited to accept the obligations of membership in the League for the purposes of such dispute, upon such conditions as the Council may deem just. If such invitation is accepted, the provisions of Articles 12 to 16 inclusive shall be applied with such modifications as may be deemed necessary by the Council.

Upon such invitation being given the Council shall immediately institute an inquiry into the circumstances of the dispute and recommend such action as may seem best and most effectual in the circumstances.

If a State so invited shall refuse to accept the obligations of membership in the League for the purposes of such dispute, and shall resort to war against a Member of the League, the provisions of Article 16 shall be applicable as against the State taking such action.

If both parties to the dispute when so invited refuse to accept the obligations of membership in the League for the purpose of such dispute, the Council may take such measures and make such recommendations as will prevent hostilities and will result in the settlement of the dispute.

ARTICLE 18

Every treaty or international engagement entered into hereafter by any Member of the League shall be forthwith registered with the Secretariat and shall as soon as possible be published by it. No such treaty or international engagement shall be binding until so registered.

ARTICLE 19

The Assembly may from time to time advise the reconsideration by Members of the League of treaties which have become inapplicable and the consideration of international conditions whose continuance might endanger the peace of the world.

ARTICLE 20

The Members of the League severally agree that this Covenant is accepted as abrogating all obligations or understandings *inter se* which are inconsistent with the terms thereof, and solemnly undertake that they will not hereafter enter into any engagements inconsistent with the terms thereof.

In case any Member of the League shall, before becoming a Member of the League, have undertaken any obligations inconsistent with the terms of this Covenant, it shall be the duty of such Member to take immediate steps to procure its release from such obligations.

ARTICLE 21

Nothing in this Covenant shall be deemed to affect the validity of international engagements,

such as treaties of arbitration or regional understandings like the Monroe doctrine, for securing
the maintenance of peace.

ARTICLE 22

To those colonies and territories which as a consequence of the late war have ceased to be under
the sovereignty of the States which formerly governed them and which are inhabited by peoples
not yet able to stand by themselves under the
strenuous conditions of the modern world, there
should be applied the principle that the well-
being and development of such peoples form a
sacred trust of civilization and that securities for
the performance of this trust should be embodied
in this Covenant.

The best method of giving practical effect to
this principle is that the tutelage of such peoples
should be entrusted to advanced nations who by
reason of their resources, their experience or their
geographical position can best undertake this responsibility, and who are willing to accept it, and
that this tutelage should be exercised by them as
Mandatories on behalf of the League.

The character of the mandate must differ according to the stage of the development of the
people, the geographical situation of the territory, its economic conditions, and other similar
circumstances.

Certain communities formerly belonging to the

Turkish Empire have reached a stage of development where their existence as independent nations can be provisionally recognized subject to the rendering of administrative advice and assistance by a Mandatory until such time as they are able to stand alone. The wishes of these communities must be a principal consideration in the selection of the Mandatory.

Other peoples, especially those of Central Africa, are at such a stage that the Mandatory must be responsible for the administration of the territory under conditions which will guarantee freedom of conscience and religion, subject only to the maintenance of public order and morals, the prohibition of abuses such as the slave trade, the arms traffic, and the liquor traffic, and the prevention of the establishment of fortifications or military and naval bases and of military training of the natives for other than police purposes and the defence of territory, and will also secure equal opportunities for the trade and commerce of other Members of the League.

There are territories, such as South-West Africa and certain of the South Pacific Islands, which, owing to the sparseness of their population, or their small size, or their remoteness from the centers of civilization, or their geographical contiguity to the territory of the Mandatory, and other circumstances, can be best administered under the laws of the Mandatory as integral portions of its territory, subject to the safeguards above mentioned in the interests of the indigenous population.

In every case of mandate, the Mandatory shall render to the Council an annual report in reference to the territory committed to its charge.

The degree of authority, control, or administration to be exercised by the Mandatory shall, if not previously agreed upon by the Members of the League, be explicitly defined in each case by the Council.

A permanent Commission shall be constituted to receive and examine the annual reports of the Mandatories and to advise the Council on all matters relating to the observance of the mandates.

ARTICLE 23

Subject to and in accordance with the provisions of international conventions existing or hereafter to be agreed upon, the Members of the League:

(a) will endeavour to secure and maintain fair and humane conditions of labor for men, women, and children, both in their own countries and in all countries to which their commercial and industrial relations extend, and for that purpose will establish and maintain the necessary international organizations;

(b) undertake to secure just treatment of the

native inhabitants of territories under their
control;

(c) will entrust the League with the general
supervision over the execution of agreements
with regard to the traffic in women and children, and the traffic in opium and other dangerous drugs;

(d) will entrust the League with the general
supervision of the trade in arms and ammunition with the countries in which the control of this traffic is necessary in the common
interest;

(e) will make provision to secure and maintain
freedom of communications and of transit
and equitable treatment for the commerce of
all Members of the League. In this connection, the special necessities of the regions
devastated during the war of 1914–1918
shall be borne in mind;

(f) will endeavor to take steps in matters of international concern for the prevention and
control of disease.

ARTICLE 24

There shall be placed under the direction of the
League all international bureaux already established by general treaties if the parties to such
treaties consent. All such international bureaux
and all commissions for the regulation of matters
of international interest hereafter constituted
shall be placed under the direction of the League.

APPENDIX F

In all matters of international interest which are regulated by general conventions but which are not placed under the control of international bureaux or commissions, the Secretariat of the League shall, subject to the consent of the Council and if desired by the parties, collect and distribute all relevant information and shall render any other assistance which may be necessary or desirable.

The Council may include as part of the expenses of the Secretariat the expenses of any bureau or commission which is placed under the direction of the League.

ARTICLE 25

The Members of the League agree to encourage and promote the establishment and cooperation of duly authorized voluntary national Red Cross organizations having as purposes the improvement of health, the prevention of disease, and the mitigation of suffering throughout the world.

ARTICLE 26

Amendments to this Covenant will take effect when ratified by the Members of the League whose representatives compose the Council and by a majority of the Members of the League whose Representatives compose the Assembly.

No such amendment shall bind any Member of the League which signifies its dissent therefrom, but in that case it shall cease to be a Member of the League.

APPENDIX F

ANNEX

1. ORIGINAL MEMBERS OF THE LEAGUE OF NATIONS SIGNATORIES OF THE TREATY OF PEACE

UNITED STATES OF
    AMERICA
BELGIUM
BOLIVIA
BRAZIL
BRITISH EMPIRE
  CANADA
  AUSTRALIA
  SOUTH AFRICA
  NEW ZEALAND
  INDIA
CHINA
CUBA
ECUADOR
FRANCE
GREECE
GUATEMALA

HAITI
HEDJAZ
HONDURAS
ITALY
JAPAN
LIBERIA
NICARAGUA
PANAMA
PERU
POLAND
PORTUGAL
ROUMANIA
SERB-CROAT-SLOVENE
    STATE
SIAM
CZECHO-SLOVAKIA
URUGUAY

STATES INVITED TO ACCEDE TO THE COVENANT

ARGENTINE REPUBLIC
CHILI
COLOMBIA
DENMARK
NETHERLANDS
NORWAY
PARAGUAY

PERSIA
SALVADOR
SPAIN
SWEDEN
SWITZERLAND
VENEZUELA

APPENDIX F

2. FIRST SECRETARY GENERAL OF THE LEAGUE OF NATIONS

The Honourable Sir James Eric DRUMMOND, K.C.M.G., C.B.